LINDBERGH

LINDBERGH
TRIUMPH AND TRAGEDY

RICHARD BAK

Taylor Trade Publishing
Dallas, Texas

Copyright © 2000 by Richard Bak

Designed by David Timmons

Published by Taylor Publishing Company
1550 West Mockingbird Lane
Dallas, Texas 75235
www.taylorpub.com

Library of Congress Cataloging-in-Publication Data
Bak, Richard, 1954–
    Lindbergh : Triumph and Tragedy / by Richard Bak.
        p.   cm.
    ISBN 0-87833-246-4
    1. Lindbergh, Charles A. (Charles Augustus), 1902–1974. 2. Air pilots—United States
Biography. I. Title.
    TL540.L5B35 200
    629.13'092—dc21
    [B]
                                     99-38311
                                     CIP

10 9 8 7 6 5 4 3 2 1

Printed in the United States of America

To the memory of
Edward Allen Reckinger
1954–2000
A good man, a good father

The life of an aviator seemed to me ideal. It involved skill. It commanded adventure. It made use of the latest developments of science. I was glad I failed my college course. Mechanical engineers were fettered to factories and drafting boards, while pilots had the freedom of wind in the expanse of sky. I could spiral the desolation of a mountain peak, explore caverns of a cloud, or land on a city flying field and there convince others of aviation's future. There were times in an airplane when it seemed I had partially escaped mortality, to look down on earth like a god.

CHARLES A. LINDBERGH JR.

LINDBERGH
(THE EAGLE OF THE U.S.A)

by HOWARD JOHNSON & AL SHERMAN

Contents

LINDBERGH

Charles A. Lindbergh and his father, Congressman C. A. Lindbergh, in 1910.

CHAPTER ONE

Junior

Charles Lindbergh's legendary loathing for the media took root in the spring of 1927, when the unheralded aviator from the Midwest suddenly found himself dealing with a pack of fascinated but wildly irresponsible big-city reporters. "Depending on which paper I pick up," he later complained in *The Spirit of St. Louis*, "I find that I was born in Minnesota, that I was born in Michigan, that I was born in Nebraska; that I learned to fly at Omaha, that I learned to fly at Lincoln, that I learned to fly at San Antonio . . ." The inaccuracies and fabrications concerning his background galled Lindbergh—a notorious stickler for detail—as he tried to stay focused on his attempt to fly solo across the Atlantic. But it was a blessing for the young pilot's universally wholesome image that, at the time, neither he nor the sensationalistic press corps knew the full particulars of his ancestry. For the Lindbergh story begins with a Swede on the lam.

One day in 1859, Ola Mansson crossed the Detroit River from Canada into the United States, looking for a fresh start. The fifty-one-year-old immigrant, accompanied by his new young wife and their year-old child, desperately needed one, because the life he had left behind in Sweden was a mess. An unschooled dairy farmer who had risen to become a radical in the *Riksdag*, the Swedish parliament, Mansson had been in the middle of a promising, albeit contentious, political career as a social reformer when he self-destructed.

Mansson spent much of the year in Stockholm. While his wife and eight children remained on their Baltic farm six hundred miles away, Mansson shared his free time in the capital with a pretty waitress named Lovisa Callen, who was twenty-seven years his junior. In 1858 Lovisa had a son by Mansson. He was named Karl August (after the new king) and duly registered in Stockholm's book of bastards.

Mansson now had to financially support two families. Perhaps not coincidentally, the following year he stood accused of embezzlement, the result of accepting small commissions in return for helping to secure loans in his position as an officer of the State Bank of Sweden. Although the accusation was brought by one of Mansson's many politically conservative enemies, the charge stood up under formal investigation. But when the Supreme Court of Sweden formally stripped Mansson of his civil rights in June 1859, the disgraced defendant had already acquired a passport, taken some rudimentary English language courses, provided for his wife and children by legally transferring his property to his oldest son, and fled Sweden with his mistress and their eighteen-month-old baby.

Ola Mansson and his mistress, Lovisa, fled Sweden in 1859 and started a new life in Minnesota as August and Louisa Lindbergh. In this family portrait from the 1870s, their first child, Charles August Lindbergh (Charles Lindbergh's father), stands at right.

Carrying a minimum of belongings, the trio embarked on an arduous ten-week journey through England, Canada, and the United States before finally settling into a crude sod house in Melrose, Minnesota, near Sauk Centre. By now Mansson had changed his name. Exchanging Ola for Augustus, and then borrowing from the Swedish words for mountain and the linden tree—a species frequently used for ornamental planting in the Old World and the New—he constructed a new identity: August Lindbergh. Lovisa became Louisa Lindbergh, while their son's name was anglicized to Charles August Lindbergh.

His scandalous past behind him, August Lindbergh faced the rigors of the Minnesota frontier with characteristic resolve and gumption.

At no time was his pluck more evident than when he suffered a near fatal sawmill accident just two years after arriving in Minnesota. While delivering some logs to be cut into planks for the new frame house he was building, August somehow stumbled into a running saw. The blade carved off a chunk of his left arm and sliced deep enough into his back that horrified witnesses could see his heart beating through the gaping wound.

"It was hot weather and there was no surgeon within fifty miles," recalled Reverend C. S. Harrison, who helped load Lindbergh onto a cart. "I followed him to his home and we did not think that he could live. I picked out the sawdust and rags from his wound and kept the mangled arm wrapped in cold water."

It was three days before a doctor finally arrived. Lindbergh remained stoic and uncomplaining throughout the ordeal, calmly applying pressure to stop the bleeding and directing Louisa and young Charles to bring cold, fresh spring water to bathe his injuries and to keep his fever down. August's arm was amputated at the shoulder and his back wound sewn up. Afterwards, at his request, his severed limb was brought to him inside a small wooden box. He solemnly shook the bad hand with his good, saying, "You have been a good friend to me for fifty years. But you can't be with me anymore. So good-bye. Good-bye, my friend." Once recovered, the enterprising patient devised a harness that allowed him to swing a scythe. He also grew a long, shaggy beard, which he frequently employed as a makeshift towel for his remaining hand.

Over the next thirty years, August and his growing family (he and Louisa would have seven more children) scratched out a living on two hundred acres of land. Catastrophies were a regular feature of the frontier. The 1862 Sioux uprising left hundreds of settlers dead and forced the Lindberghs to temporarily flee to St. Cloud for safety. For three straight years during the 1870s, swarms of grasshoppers reduced their carefully cultivated fields to stubble. And whooping cough claimed three of their children.

Lindbergh's maternal grandparents, Charles H. Land and Evangeline Lodge, were photographed in different Detroit studios circa 1875.

Money was hard to come by. As a result, nearly every necessity—from clothes and soap to tools and bullets—was homemade. When the family cow died, Louisa had to sell her treasured gold watch in order to buy another. From a very early age, Charles's job was to provide meat for the table. Because of the need to preserve precious ammunition, the boy developed into a crack shot. The independence and solitude of tramping the fields and streams alone agreed with the handsome, moody youth, who did not set foot inside a classroom until he was twelve years old. "I had become so imbued with the grandeur of God's Creation that, when a school was started, I could not divert my attention from Nature to books," he later said of his first experiences with formal education.

Nonetheless, Charles thrived intellectually, emphasizing the independence of thought and action that was already a Lindbergh trademark. While his father became involved in local concerns like the school board and also served as town clerk, postmaster, and justice of the peace, Charles expanded his mind at a private academy in Sauk Centre, then moved on to the University of Michigan, where he earned his law degree in 1883. It was there that Charles gained his nickname, "C. A.," from his habit of signing papers with his first two initials.

By the time August died in 1892, C. A. was married and enjoying success as a lawyer and a realtor in Little Falls, about fifty miles from where he grew up. He and the former Mary LaFond had two children, Lillian and Eva, a handsome brick house, and high standing in the community. The young attorney was much admired for his

Evangeline Lodge Land, Charles Lindbergh's mother, circa 1900.

principled and common sensical approach to life and the law. Like his father, he believed in fostering self reliance. A favorite expression when counseling someone with a problem was: "Now, you have a head, haven't you?"

In the spring of 1898, C. A. was settled into an agreeable routine of challenging professional work and domestic bliss when his pregnant wife was unexpectedly diagnosed with an abdominal tumor. Both Mary and the baby died. Distraught, C. A. sent his two daughters to live with relatives in Minneapolis, then moved into the local Antlers Hotel. Taking a room at the same time was the new science teacher at Little Falls High School, twenty-four-year-old Evangeline Lodge Land. "He was an Apollo for physical beauty," Evangeline's uncle, John C. Lodge, observed of the tall, chiseled widower, "and my niece was soon swept off her feet."

Evangeline Lodge Land descended from two of the most prominent families in nineteenth-century Detroit. Her mother, Evangeline Lodge, was one of eleven siblings, several of whom became physicians. Her father, Dr. Charles Land, was an eccentric dentist who pioneered the controversial use of porcelain in dentistry, a technique that brought him ridicule, professional ostracism, and financial woes as he engaged in an ongoing series of lawsuits. Dr. Land's unconventional views extended to the education of women. He sent his daughter to the University of Michigan, where she graduated in 1899 with a degree in chemistry.

With her blue eyes and striking figure, Evangeline Lodge Land had been considered by many to be the most attractive coed on campus. Moreover, she exhibited the kind of adventuresome spirit and independence of thought that naturally appealed to someone like C. A. Lindbergh. Resisting suggestions that she teach school in Detroit, she had dreamily decided to "go to some mining town and teach chemistry to the children of miners." At first a $55-a-month job in a one-room schoolhouse in Little Falls seemed to fit the fantasy. But after just a few months of rotating between the classroom and her hotel room, the disillusioned transplant wrote her family that Little Falls "shall not see so very much more of this chicken."

Falling in love with the handsome and prosperous C. A. Lindbergh changed her mind. After a suitable period of courtship, they became man and wife at her parents' place in Detroit on March 27, 1901. Following a California honeymoon, they settled into the house C. A. had built for them on a 120-acre site in the Minnesota countryside. It was more of an estate than a farm. C. A. had even given it a name, "Lindholm," which had to please his refined wife. The impressively appointed three-story, thirteen-room house sat on a bluff above the Mississippi River and was surrounded by oak, elm, and linden trees. It was a magnificent setting, the young bride remembered, the solitude made musical by birdsong and the muffled sound of rushing water.

Evangeline soon became pregnant. She made it clear that a Swedish midwife was out of the question. She returned to her parents' house in Detroit, where she was tended to by her great-uncle, Dr. Edwin Lodge. At one-thirty in the morning of February 4, 1902, Uncle Edwin helped Evangeline deliver a healthy nine-and-a-half-

Charles Lindbergh was born inside this house at 258 West Forest in Detroit on February 4, 1902. This photograph was taken in 1927, by which time the street address had been renumbered to 1120. The house was torn down in 1973.

pound boy. The baby's blue eyes drew comment, as did his large feet. He was named Charles Augustus Lindbergh Jr., a slight variation of his father's name, Charles August. To help keep the two Charles A. Lindberghs straight, the boy often would be referred to as "Junior."

•   •   •

Charles Jr., was six weeks old when he began living at Lindholm. His second-story bedroom window afforded views of the natural world that produced some of his earliest and finest memories. Depending on the hour or the season, he could gaze on stars shining like a shower of new dimes, pick out figures and faces in the billowing clouds, or watch formations of geese imperturbably winging west through a pewter sky. The house burned down one terrible day in 1906. The youngster, pulled to safety by the

The future aviator and his mother in 1902.

family nurse, watched the conflagration and thought, "Where is my father—my mother—what will happen to my toys?" The house and toys were soon replaced. But the fire served as an unintentional metaphor for his parents' relationship, which unbeknownst to him was also crumbling into ashes.

More significant than the fifteen-year age difference between C. A. and Evangeline was their conflicting temperaments. Where C. A. was stoic and undemonstrative, Evangeline was given to sudden mood swings. She was later described by her son as having "highly charged and unpredictable" emotions, a person who during one particularly rancorous exchange with her husband put a loaded pistol to his head. Then there was Evangeline's imperious manner. Throughout her long life, no matter what the setting, she seldom missed an opportunity to demonstrate her social or intellectual superiority. In her view, the only things cultivated about the Minnesotans she casually lumped together as "Swede farmers" were their crops. She rarely associated with them and frowned on her son doing the same.

Contributing to the household tension was the presence of young Charles's stepsisters, Lillian and Eva, who were fourteen and nine, respectively, when C. A. remarried. The girls, who had been staying with various relatives, happily reunited with their father. But they never warmed to Evangeline, whose arrogant assurance and arbitrary rages, coupled with her inexperience in childrearing and obvious devotion to her own child, made her a poor stepmother. The girls' relationship with Evangeline grew more contentious as they blossomed into strong-willed young women of their own. "She made life miserable for all of us," was Eva's recollection many years later.

During the early years of marriage C. A. had become increasingly interested in politics, though he initially resisted all attempts to get him to run for office. By 1906 he'd had a change of heart. That fall he campaigned for a Congressional seat and convincingly beat the two-time incumbent. As the new Republican representative from the Sixth District of Minnesota, C. A. railed against the bankers and other "money interests" growing fat on the labor of small farmers, a fight he kept up through five terms in office.

The Lindberghs moved to Washington in the fall of 1907, with Charles, wearing a sailor's suit, accompanying his father to the opening of the Sixtieth Congress. Aside from the thrill of seeing his father sworn in that day, the youngster disliked nearly everything about the nation's capital: the absence of trees to climb, fish to catch and meadows to run in, the proliferation of soot and noise. One day C. A. came home from a legislative session and took Charles for a walk. After returning to the apartment the boy started punching and bothering his father.

high on the door. Still there. He said, "I was foolish. I wasn't thinking whether or not there were any other people in the house."

His dad bought a 1916 Saxon. Before that he had a Model T. He taught Charles how to drive a car when he was twelve. He had great confidence in Charles because he was responsible and did a lot of thinking before he did something. He rarely did foolish things. That's why his flight to Paris was so successful, because he did a lot of thinking about it, a lot of planning. When Charles was just fourteen his father permitted him to drive his mother and uncle to California. Now, it took him forty days because you know in 1916 the roads were very rough. Had a lot of flat tires and so on. But they made the trip to California in good shape and a few months later they came back with Charles driving the whole way. Didn't even have a driver's license.

That old Saxon was in the garage for years. It rusted out. After the flight some people around here took it out, put it on the back of a truck in a parade that they had for Lindbergh when he visited Little Falls after his flight to Paris. And they had a big sign: "Charlie's First Plane."

After that, some fellows from the National Guard stationed at Fort Ripley, Minnesota, took the old car and they refurbished it completely. Worked on it for months, getting parts from all over the country. The top was gone, the hood was gone, and so on. But they got it in running condition and used it in a lot of parades. So when Lindbergh came in 1971 I took him down to the garage and showed him that car and he was

Lindbergh at the wheel of the family Saxon, 1971.

delighted. He remembered that car in its terrible condition. He got in and he sat down. I got a picture of him at the wheel and he's got a big smile on his face. He said, "This is the first time in fifty years that I've sat in this car." It was a great moment for him. He remembered taking his dad around the state when he was running for the Senate. His father hardly ever drove. When he wanted to go some place, he'd say, "Charles, take me over to so-and-so." And he would.

Want to know how Lindbergh learned how to swim? Well, right by the house in the Mississippi River, there is a big rock—oh, I'd say thirty or forty feet from shore. One day—Charles must have been nine or ten at the time—his father got him on his back and swam out to that rock. After they sat on the rock for a while, his father said, "Charles, I want you to swim back to shore." So he put Charles back in the water. He splashed and paddled and he finally discovered he could float and he swam back to shore. While all this was going on, his father stayed on the rock. That's how much confidence he had in his son. He wasn't scared at all that Charles might go under or drown.

After a day or two here Lindbergh got a call from back east. He was a member of the Pan American board of directors and they were having a very important meeting. Lindbergh told me, "I have to fly back. If you could get me down to Minneapolis I'll take a flight to New York. As soon as I can I'll come back and pick up the Volkswagen." About a year later he sent me a package with a new license for the VW and he said, "I'll be back to pick it up one of these days." He never did. After a couple of years he said, "Why don't you keep it?" So we did. It's still there in the garage, along with the Saxon.

The last time he visited Little Falls was in the winter of '72. I asked him, "General, you've lost some weight. Is that on purpose?" I called him General because that was his rank in the reserves. He said, "No, I caught a virus in Switzerland." He and Anne had a little chalet in Switzerland, you know. And he changed the subject. I found out later that doctors had discovered he had cancer of the lymphatic system. He never told anyone, not even his wife. Finally he went to the hospital in New York because he was sick. That was the only time he was hospitalized since he had measles as a boy. Anne was mad as hell. He said, "Well, I didn't want to have you worrying about me so I never told you."

When we got word that he died we advertised a memorial service. Hundreds of people came. It was held on the screened front porch, where he had slept on hot summer nights and where he'd run in and out of so many times as a youth. To listen to him talk, those were the happiest days of his life.

Lindbergh with fellow barnstormer Bud Gurney, circa 1924.

CHAPTER TWO

Plane Crazy

Lindbergh reported to Lincoln Standard Aircraft the first week of April
1922 and immediately began learning aviation from the ground up.
Inside the hangar he helped tear down engines and learned to "dope" the
fabric skin with a waterproof varnish—routine chores to veteran pilots,
but endlessly fascinating to Charles.

On Saturday, April 9, the newcomer and a sixteen-year-old Lincoln Standard
employee named Harland "Bud" Gurney went on their first airplane ride together.
The pair squeezed into the front cockpit of one of the company's reconditioned army
training planes (dubbed "Tourabouts") while the chief engineer, Otto Timm, revved
the engine, checked the instruments and wind direction, then taxied down the sod
field before lifting off into space. After a fifteen-minute flight over the Nebraska countryside, the trio safely returned to earth.

Charles was euphoric. The experience changed his life forever.

"My early flying seemed an experience beyond mortality," he wrote a half-century
later. "There was the earth spreading out below me, a planet where I had lived but
from which I had astonishingly risen. It had been the home of my body. I felt strangely
apart from my body in the plane. I was never more aware of all existence, never less
aware of myself. Mine was a god's-eye view."

A crusty ex-army flight instructor, Ira Biffle, gave Lindbergh his first flying
lessons. Demonstrating exceptional eyesight and reflexes, the student was a quick
learner. "The actual flying of the ship is easy, also the take-off," he observed at the
time. "But the landing is Hell." Biffle was unmoved by Lindbergh's obvious enthusiasm for instruction. He had been badly shaken by the recent death of his best friend in
a crash and had soured on the profession. Besides, company owner Ray Page had
promised to sell the training plane to a local barnstorming pilot, Erold Bahl. Page
couldn't risk having a novice damage the craft—which, like all airplanes then, was
uninsured—in a crack-up of his own. The result is that Lindbergh spent only eight
hours inside a cockpit before convincing Bahl to bring him along as his assistant.

In these early years of aviation, barnstorming was a popular and often lucrative
occupation. A gypsy pilot would literally fly in and out of town at tree-top level, stopping just long enough to give adventurous farmers a five-minute ride for five bucks
apiece before moving on to the next village or county fair. Stunts such as wing-walking
and parachute jumping often were employed to attract larger crowds.

The principals of the barnstorming act that toured Kansas, Nebraska, Colorado, Wyoming, and Montana during the summer of 1922. From left: Banty Rogers, Lindbergh, H. J. "Shorty" Lynch, and Rogers's death-defying fox terrier, Booster.

One day in the middle of Bahl's month-long tour of Nebraska, Kansas, and Colorado, Charles suggested standing on the wing and waving as a way of wowing potential customers.

"You can climb out of the cockpit if you want to," replied Bahl, "but watch your step on the spars, and don't go farther than the inner-bay strut the first time."

The rubber-legged novice did as he was told, carefully edging a short way out onto the wing before halting to wave a sweaty hand to the wide-eyed crowds. Wing-walking never really agreed with Lindbergh, who had recurring nightmares of tumbling helplessly through space. But he refused to give in to his fears, setting his jaw and stepping out each nerve-wracking time.

Daring
Feats
With
Para=
chutes

George Starr of Buffalo, N.Y., making a leap with a parachute from an airplane while flying at a height of 2,000 feet. The picture was snapped a few seconds after leaving the plane, the tail of which can be seen at the extreme left of the photograph. A stiff wind was blowing at the time, but the landing was made without injury.

Largest parachute in the world, capable of carrying ten men, each weighing 200 pounds, designed for use from the basket of a high-altitude type of balloon, photographed just prior to its test at McCook Field, Dayton, Ohio. The experience in the World War and the rapid growth of aviation for all purposes, sporting and commercial, has stimulated invention in this most important adjunct in case of injury to balloon or plane.

Daring girl parachute novice, Miss Ethel Dare of Chicago, landing from her first jump from an airplane flying 5,000 feet over the lake front, the strong wind dragging her some distance before the parachute could be controlled.

This page from a 1922 newspaper illustrates the skydiving exploits of a pair of daredevils, George Starr and the appropriately named Ethel Dare.

These snapshots of female stunt pilot Lillian Boyer were taken in 1922, the same year "Aerial Daredevil Lindbergh" started to make a name for himself on the barnstorming circuit.

He didn't truly exorcise his terror until he hooked up with the husband-wife duo of Charlie and Kathryn Hardin in June 1922. By now Charles was back at Lincoln Standard, making $15 a week in Ray Page's airplane factory. The Hardins made and sold parachutes, and to advertise the quality and reliability of their product they engaged in all kinds of breathtaking aerial stunts. These included a double parachute jump, a maneuver that saw the jumper deploy one chute, cut away the canopy, then free fall several seconds before a string attached to the first chute yanked open the second. From the moment Lindbergh saw Charlie Hardin fling himself off a wing, two thousand feet above the ground, only to float back to earth under a billowing cloud of muslin, he knew he had to attempt the same feat.

"I want to jump," he informed Charlie Hardin one June day, "and I'd like to make it a double jump."

Hardin was incredulous. "A double jump! You want to do a double jump the *first* time?"

Lindbergh assured him that he did. Late the following afternoon Hardin took him up eighteen hundred feet above Lincoln. At that point the lanky beginner gingerly walked out to the very end of the wing, attached his harness to the chute bag, and then dropped over the side.

At first, all seemed well. The parachute opened, arresting Charles's descent, and after a few seconds he cut the shrouds away from his harness. Then he waited for the second chute, which was attached to the first by a length of twine, to deploy. He waited . . . and waited. . . . The next thing he knew he was spiraling headfirst towards the earth, wondering what in God's name had happened. Finally, just as it appeared to those on the ground that their free-falling companion would leave a bigger impression on Nebraska than he intended, the second chute filled with rushing air and blossomed with a gratifying rustle. Afterward, Charles learned that the usually reliable Hardin had tied the two chutes together with cheap grocery-store string, which had snapped, resulting in his near-fatal fall.

For the rest of his life, Charles never tired of talking or writing about his first jump, for it purged him of his dark phobia. "Strangely enough," he later said, "I've never fallen in my dreams since I actually fell through air."

A mechanic, a budding pilot, a wing walker, and now a parachute jumper—the twenty-year-old Lindbergh found himself a valuable commodity. That summer he joined a local pilot named H. J. "Shorty" Lynch for a barnstorming tour of Kansas,

"It's a sociable place, under a wing," Lindbergh once reflected. Here "Slim" Lindbergh (kneeling, center) enjoys the camaraderie of several pilots and mechanics at some undisclosed location during his nomadic barnstorming days.

C. A. Lindbergh (far left) examines the damage to his son's Jenny on June 8, 1923, after the plane ran into a ditch on takeoff from a farm field outside Glencoe, Minnesota. The senior Lindbergh was running for a U.S. Senate seat.

Nebraska, Wyoming, and Montana. Promoted as "Aerial Daredevil Lindbergh," his seemingly suicidal stunts actually were well thought out and thus of negligible risk. "The day I stood on the top wing of an airplane while it looped, I was tied on as safely as though I'd been strapped in my cockpit," he recalled of the heel cups, wire cable and harness that, invisible to spectators, held him in place.

Although always a modest person when it came to his accomplishments, Lindbergh quietly enjoyed the deference given him. "Ranchers, cowboys, storekeepers in town, followed with their eyes as I walked by. Had I been the ghost of 'Liver-Eating Johnson' I could hardly have been accorded more prestige. Shooting and gunplay those people understood, but a man who'd willingly jump off an airplane's wing had a disdain for death that was beyond them."

The tour ended in October in Montana. Although he had yet to solo, he had spent six months in, under, around, and on top of airplanes and had loved every minute of it. Life would be even more delicious once he owned his own plane—a goal he shared with his mother. "You know what you want," responded Evangeline, who wondered: "has the occupation of pilot any future?" The year 1922 turned out to be an eventful one for Evangeline as well. After doing graduate work at Columbia University, she returned to Detroit. Upon her father's death in August, she decided to remain in her home town. She took a job teaching chemistry at the city's leading high school, Cass Technical, and moved in with her bachelor brother, Charles.

During the winter of 1922–23, Lindbergh spent a good deal of time with his father in Minneapolis, where C. A. was attempting to start a law practice. The aging quixote's post-Congressional life had mostly been a succession of political and financial setbacks. He had self-published books attacking those old bogeymen, bankers and war profiteers, started a newspaper, and speculated in Florida real estate. Since leaving office he had deteriorated, both physically and mentally, walking around in unkempt clothes and often appearing confused or melancholic. Nonetheless, as Charles

Lindbergh snapped this photograph of his mother in 1923, the year she accompanied him on several of his barnstorming stops. Later, she occasionally would be a passenger on his air mail runs, enjoying the ride while sitting atop a pile of mail sacks.

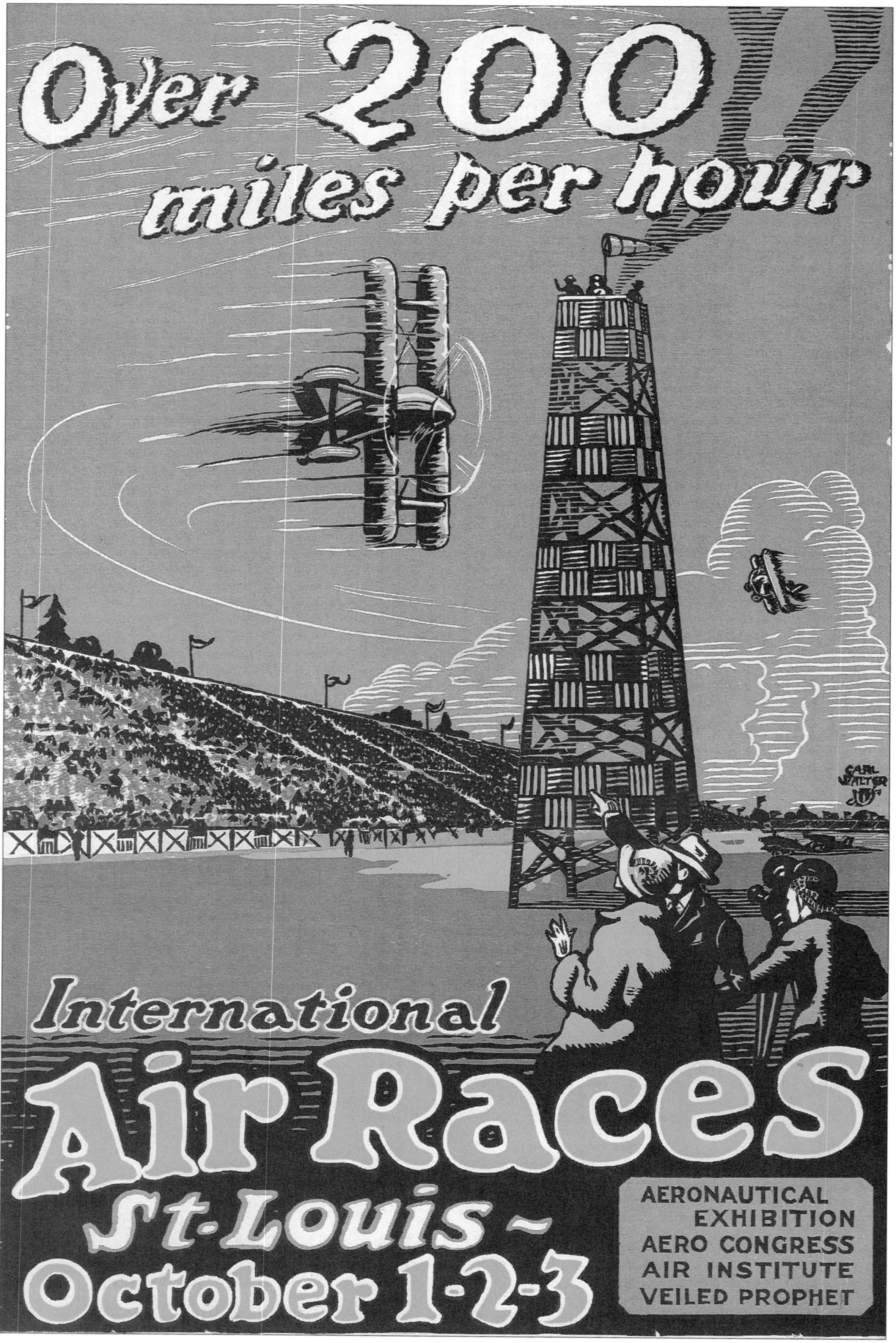
Over 200 miles per hour
International
Air Races
St. Louis ~
October 1-2-3
AERONAUTICAL EXHIBITION
AERO CONGRESS
AIR INSTITUTE
VEILED PROPHET
CARL WALTER

St. Louis's Lambert Field, built on the site of a cornfield, hosted the 1923 air races.

Automobile dealer Leon Klink (left) owned the Canuck in which Lindbergh flew a barnstorming tour over the winter of 1923–1924, just prior to his entering the Army flying school.

approached his twenty-first birthday, C. A. had enough on the ball to recognize the quality of the boy he and Evangeline had raised. "He is in splendid condition," he wrote her, "and exercises the most sense of one of his age that I have ever taken notice of."

C. A. was quietly nervous, and slightly disappointed, over his son's choice of careers. He offered to help set him up in a safer, more respectable profession. However, when Charles couldn't come up with the entire $500 needed to buy his first plane, a war-surplus Curtiss JN4-D "Jenny," C. A. secured a loan. Jennies were unstable, had a top speed of 70 miles per hour, and lacked brakes, but they were the popular choice of the growing number of barnstormers zig-zagging the countryside after the war.

In late April, Charles traveled to Souther Field in Americus, Georgia, to take delivery. There was a problem, he recalled. "Everybody at Souther Field took for granted that I was an experienced pilot when I arrived alone to buy a plane. They didn't ask to see my license, because you didn't have to have a license to fly an airplane in 1923."

Charles had never soloed. In fact, at this point he had less than ten hours' flying time, all of it operating dual controls with an instructor on board. His inexperience became embarrassingly clear on his first takeoff, which he quickly aborted after the plane had climbed just a few feet into the air. The Jenny landed drunkenly on one wheel, the wing tip skidding across the clay.

A young pilot named Henderson was watching and came to his rescue. He suggested the two of them practice a few takeoffs and landings until Charles felt comfortable with the controls. By five that afternoon Lindbergh was ready to attempt it alone. "No matter how much training you've had," he would say of that moment, "your first solo is far different from all other flights. You are completely independent, hopelessly beyond help, entirely responsible, and terribly alone in space." Charles spent the next week at Souther Field, perfecting his takeoffs and landings, before lumbering off in the underpowered Jenny to join his father in Minnesota.

At sixty-three, the senior Lindbergh still had one last adventure left in him. Senator Knute Nelson had recently died in office, causing a special election to be held to fill the vacancy. C. A. hit the campaign trail, assisted by his flyboy son. Although in Charles's view his father was probably terrified every minute he spent aloft, the candidate gamely flew from stop to stop, an itinerary that included an unscheduled crackup in a rutted field outside Glencoe. C. A. should have taken the crash as an omen; he finished a distant third in the polls.

While C. A. returned to Minneapolis, Charles gravitated toward Lambert Field in St. Louis, Missouri. The converted cornfield had become the crossroads of American aviation, a distinction reinforced by its hosting of the 1923 International Air Races that October. Lindbergh, arriving in his ancient Jenny, felt conspicuously inferior among the many nationally known pilots and their high-powered aircraft—"like a forty-acre farmer stumbling through a state fair," he later confessed.

During the meet he ran into Bud Gurney, his friend from the Nebraska days. Gurney had already won a parachute-jumping contest and needed a pilot for the double-drop competition. Charles agreed to take him up. Unfortunately, Gurney exited poorly and wound up breaking his arm and shoulder. Lindbergh "took it worse than I did," Gurney said later. "It wasn't his fault. It was my carelessness. But he kept blaming himself for my heavy fall—and he insisted on giving me a stake for when I got out of the hospital." Charles had a little money to spare; the day before the accident he had arranged to sell his Jenny at a small profit to a young Iowan in exchange for a down payment, and a promissory note for the balance. To seal the deal, Lindbergh threw in some flying lessons, with a solo flight guaranteed.

It was during this period—with his partner in the hospital, his plane sold, cold weather setting in, barnstorming drying up, and job prospects in civil aviation practically nonexistent—that Charles chewed over a local pilot's advice. Lambert Field was the home base of the 110th Observation Squad of the Missouri National Guard. "Why don't you sign up with the Army as an air cadet? You get all the flying you want—and they pay you for it."

Lindbergh had never abandoned his adolescent dream of flying a scout plane for Uncle Sam. Given his wanderlust and distaste for classrooms, the regimentation and studying didn't figure to agree with him, but he longed to fly the powerful aircraft available to military pilots. At the Air Races, a Navy Curtiss biplane with a D-12 engine had won the Pulitzer Trophy Race with an average speed of nearly 244 miles per hour. And unlike his Jenny, which could barely bump the underside of clouds, the Army's De Havillands could climb to more than 12,000 feet. In late 1923 Lindbergh applied to the War Department for admission to the one-year aviation training program, then a few weeks later took the required mental and physical examinations.

Lambert Field, St. Louis, April 15, 1926: Lindbergh is ceremoniously handed the first sack of air mail as Robertson Aircraft inaugurates service between St. Louis and Chicago.

Next I turned my attention to locating a landing place. I was over mesquite and drifting in the general direction of a plowed field which I reached by slipping the chute. Shortly before striking the ground, I was drifting backwards, but was able to swing around in the harness just as I landed on the side of a ditch 100 feet from the edge of the mesquite. Although the impact of landing was too great for me to remain standing, I was not injured in any way. The parachute was still held open by the wind and did not collapse until I pulled in one group of shroud lines.

During my descent I lost my goggles, a vest-pocket camera which fitted tightly in my hip pocket, and the rip-cord of the parachute.

Lieut. Maughan landed his DH in the field and took our chutes back to Kelly. Twenty minutes later Captain Guidera brot [sic] a DH and a chute over for me and I returned to Kelly Field with him.

An hour after the crash we were flying in another nine-ship S.E. 5 formation with two new S.E. 5's.

The narrative is striking in a couple of respects. As a literary document it is an exemplar of conciseness and attention to detail, so much so that it was reprinted in *Aviation Magazine* and the *New York Evening Herald* (Lindbergh's first published prose) and, after he became famous, was used as a teaching aid in English classrooms. More remarkable is what it says about Charles's coolness in the face of grave danger, for his laconic writing style was of a piece with his matter-of-fact approach to the perils of flying. No mistake about it, aviation was extremely dangerous, a reality driven home by the nearly daily news reports of crashes and pilot deaths in one part of the world or another. At the time the estimated lifespan of an aviator was roughly 900 flying hours. But Charles had already made a pact, of sorts, with the devil. Back in Nebraska he had decided that if he could fly for ten years before dying in a crash, then "it would be a worthwhile trade for an ordinary lifetime."

Charles's life remained anything but ordinary after graduation. The freshly minted Lieutenant Lindbergh moved his base of operations to Lambert Field, where he made a living as a flight instructor and barnstorming phenomenon billed as "The Flying Fool." As if performing aerial stunts wasn't dangerous enough, at times he served as a test pilot, on one ocassion narrowly surviving the crash of an experimental four-passenger plane called the "Plywood Special" into a local potato patch. This crack-up on June 2, 1925, earned its pilot another distinction. According to an informal fraternity of lucky fliers known as the Caterpillar Club, Lindbergh was the only pilot in America known to have twice saved his life through an emergency parachute jump. He did, however, dislocate his shoulder in the fall.

By now Charles was known to just about everyone as "Slim," a moniker inspired by his bladelike figure. He stood a shade over six feet, two inches high and weighed about 150 pounds. He had a twenty-nine-inch waist. With his blue eyes, dimpled chin, and tousled hair, he had grown into a handsome young man. He was the very image of the dashing aviator and could have collected all the women he wanted. Instead, he seemed a man without vices. He didn't smoke, drink, or gamble. He had no use for curse words, his strongest expression being "Jesus Christ on a bicycle!"

"He could make you feel mighty guilty after the third beer," said Bud Gurney, "and didn't approve at all of girl-chasing, which was something every other youngster around indulged in. On the other hand, he was always a great one for risque jokes, and some of them he told came quite close to the bone."

Lindbergh's affection for practical jokes has perhaps been overstated, but the pranks serve to soften the humorless and reserved image that a lifetime of serious pursuits helped create. One day at Lambert Field, for example, he filled a water bucket with kerosene, as literal a "gag" as poor Bud Gurney—who took two deep swallows of the stuff before realizing what he was drinking—ever experienced. Then there was the infamous "painted penis" episode from his army days. As Lindbergh recalled:

> One of the cadets in my class at Brooks Field frequently patronized the brothels in San Antonio's "Spick Town." He was a huge man and he used to brag about his activities in Spick Town. He was an extraordinarily deep sleeper.
>
> On a hot Texas weekend afternoon, he was lying naked and asleep on top of his barracks-room bunk. He lay on his back, and his penis, proportioned to his size, was standing erect and stiff. Several cadets began discussing what action it would be appropriate to take. I suggested that we paint the penis green. (I knew where some green paint and a brush were easily available.)
>
> Our mission accomplished, the cadet remained still sleeping and still in the same condition. We then screwed a metal "eye" into the ceiling over his

bunk, passed a long string through it, fashioned a lasso at one end of the string, and ran the other end out of a window. After lassoing the penis, one cadet took station outside the window and the rest of us sat on our bunks, apparently reading or talking.

When the end of the string was pulled, the cadet woke up, rose on his elbows, and stared at his his green-painted penis. He had a grand sense of humor. All he said was "Je-sus CHRIST!"

In the fall of 1925, the U.S. government awarded the first Contract Air Mail routes. CAM-2, the Chicago-to-St. Louis run, went to the Robertson brothers, Frank and William. Lindbergh, widely regarded as one of the finest pilots at Lambert Field, now had one of the best jobs in civil aviation: flying the mail as the $200-a-month chief pilot of the Robertson Aircraft Corporation. Over the next several months he helped lay out the 285-mile run, establishing nine primitive airfields in towns like Peoria and Springfield along the way. In each case the "airport" was little more than a pasture with a wind sock and access to a nearby telephone.

On the afternoon of April 15, 1926, two hundred people at Lambert Field watched as the first sacks of mail were ceremoniously loaded into the front cockpit of Lindbergh's silver-and-maroon plane. With this, Robertson Aircraft inaugurated mail service between St. Louis and Chicago.

By modern standards navigation was alarmingly primitive then, with Lindbergh and his contemporaries typically following visible landmarks below—rivers, roads, railroad tracks—to their destination. Nightfall forced a pilot to depend on moonlight, the electric glow of a distant town, or the pinpoint of a kerosene lamp in a farmhouse window to guide him. Like all of Robertson's air mail pilots, Lindbergh flew a rebuilt De Havilland with a 400-horsepower Liberty engine. It lacked landing and navigation lights, making each day's round trip especially challenging during the winter months, when daylight was at a premium. Generally speaking, air mail pilots flew as far as they could until poor visibility forced them to land. If it happened to be at one of the intermediary stops, the mail was taken off the plane and put onto the next train.

Unpredictable weather and the lack of accurate meteorological information added to the peril. Charles made two more emergency jumps as an air mail pilot, garnering him recognition as the country's only four-time "caterpillar" (and wiping out half of the Robertson brothers' fleet in the process). On the evening of September 16, 1926, he was caught in a fog northeast of Peoria, Illinois. He headed towards Chicago's Maywood Field, where ground crews, expecting his arrival, were futilely scanning the sky with searchlights. After spending nearly two hours circling in this soup and draining his main and reserve gas tanks, Lindbergh maneuvered his plane over open country and then bailed out. As he was floating to safety, the plane unexpectedly coughed back to life, passing too close for comfort before both man and machine made their separate landings in a cornfield. A month and a half later, on November 3, a sudden squall forced him to jump out somewhere between Springfield and Peoria. This time he landed on a barbed wire fence. A nickname he would soon come to hate, "Lucky Lindy," didn't originate here, but it should have. Not only was he unhurt, he didn't even suffer a tear in his flying suit.

Aside from those occasional bits of excitement, flying the same route, day after day, quickly bored Charles, as he had expected it would. He was the kind of person who not only welcomed new challenges, but thrived on them. During uneventful flights he let his mind wander. Although he had been promoted to captain in the Missouri National Guard, he'd had no luck in obtaining a regular Army commission. And despite his wide range of experience operating a variety of aircraft, he'd been unsuccessful in trying to secure a spot on one of the various aerial expeditions then being formed.

His thoughts increasingly centered on the new single-winged plane in the news, the Wright-Bellanca, and he mused about how far he might be able to fly such a beauty. "Judging from the accounts I've read, it is the most efficient plane ever built. It could break the world's endurance record, and the transcontinental, and set a dozen marks for range and speed and weight. Possibly—my mind is startled at its thought— I could fly nonstop between New York and Paris."

"SLIM" LINDBERGH

"The plane was a ball-shaped mass"

Between March 1925 and November 1926, Charles Lindbergh made four emergency parachute jumps, then an unprecedented record of escapes for American airmen. His third bail-out occurred the evening of September 16, 1926, when he was flying the mail between St. Louis and Chicago. Later, in writing his official report of the incident, he described his near-death experience in characteristically succinct but detailed language.

I took off from Lambert-St. Louis Field at 4:25 P.M. and after an uneventful trip arrived at Springfield, Ill., at 5:10 P.M. and Peoria, Ill., at 5:55 P.M.

I took off from the Peoria Field at 6:10 P.M. There was a light ground haze but the sky was practically clear, containing only scattered cumulus clouds.

Darkness set in about twenty-five miles northeast of Peoria and I took up a compass course, checking on the lights of the towns below until a low fog rolled in under me a few miles northeast of Marseilles and the Illinois River.

The fog extended from the ground up to about six hundred feet and, as I was unable to fly under it, I turned back and attempted to drop a flare and land; but the flare did not function and I again headed for Maywood [the airport in Chicago], hoping to find a break in the fog over the field.

Upon examination I discovered that the cause of the flare failure was the short length of the release lever and that the flare might still be used by pulling the release cable.

I continued on a compass course of fifty degrees until 7:15 P.M., when I saw a dull glow on top of the fog, indicating a town below.

There were several of these light patches on the fog, visible only when looking away from the moon, and I knew them to be the towns bordering the Maywood Field. At no time, however, was I able to locate the exact position of the field, although I understood that the searchlights were directed upwards and two barrels of gasoline burned in an endeavor to attract my attention.

Several times I descended to the top of the fog, which was eight to nine hundred feet high according to my altimeter. The sky above was clear with the exception of scattered clouds and the moon and stars were shining brightly.

After circling around for thirty-five minutes, I headed west to be sure of clearing Lake Michigan and in an attempt to pick up one of the lights on the transcontinental [railroad] line.

After flying west for fifteen minutes and seeing no break in the fog, I turned southwest hoping to strike the edge of the fog south of the Illinois River.

Our ships carry 110 gallons of gasoline in the main tank and about nine in the reserve, which combined should supply a Liberty motor at cruising speed for fully five hours. That would make my

time limit 9:30 P.M. and give me a twenty-minute warning of exhaustion when the main tank went dry and I switched on the reserve. Consequently, when the motor cut out at 8:20 P.M. and I cut in the reserve I expected to find low air-pressure or some other cause for cutting rather than a dry main tank. I was at the time only 1,500 feet high and as the motor did not pick up as soon as I expected I shoved the flashlight in my belt and was about to release the parachute flare and jump when the engine finally took hold again.

A second trial showed the main tank to be dry and accordingly a maximum of twenty minutes' flying time left.

Several days later, I learned that the ship was the only one equipped with an eighty-five-gallon main tank.

There were no openings in the fog and I decided to leave the ship as soon as the reserve tank was exhausted. I tried to get the mail pit open with the idea of throwing out the mail sacks and then jumping, but was unable to open the front buckle.

I knew that the risk of fire with no gasoline in the tanks was very slight and began to climb for altitude when I saw a light on the ground for several seconds. This was the first light I had seen for nearly two hours and as almost enough gasoline for fifteen minutes' flying remained in the reserve, I glided down to twelve hundred feet and pulled out the flare release cable as nearly as I could judge over the spot where the light had appeared. This time the flare functioned, but only to illuminate the top of a solid bank of fog, into which it soon disappeared without showing any trace of the ground.

Seven minutes' gasoline remained in the gravity tank. Seeing the glow of a town through the fog, I turned towards open country and nosed the plane up. At 5,000 feet the motor sputtered and died. I stepped up on the cowling and out over the right side of the cockpit, pulling the rip-cord after about a hundred-foot fall. The parachute, an Irving seat-service type, functioned perfectly. I was falling head downward when the risers jerked me into an upright position and the chute opened. This time I saved the rip-cord.

I pulled the flashlight from my belt and was playing it down towards the top of the fog when I heard the plane's motor pick up. When I jumped, the motor had practically stopped dead and I had neglected to cut the switches. Apparently when the ship nosed down an additional supply of gasoline drained down into the carburetor. Soon the ship came into sight, about a quarter of a mile away and headed in the general direction of my parachute. I put the flashlight in a pocket of my flying suit preparatory to slipping the parachute out of the way if necessary. The plane was making a left spiral of about a mile in diameter and passed approximately three hundred yards away from my chute, leaving me on the outside of the circle.

I was undecided as to whether the plane or I was descending more rapidly and glided my chute away from the spiral path of the ship as quickly as I could.

The ship passed completely out of sight, but reappeared again in a few seconds, its rate of descent being about the same as that of the parachute. I counted five spirals, each one a little farther away than the last, before reaching the top of the fog bank.

When I settled into the fog, I knew that the ground was within

Robertson Aviation's chief pilot, bundled up against the weather on one of his St. Louis-Chicago mail runs.

Lindbergh and his wrecked DH-4 after running out of fuel in heavy fog over Chicago on the night of September 15, 1926.

1,000 feet and reached for the flashlight but found it missing. I could see neither earth nor stars and had no idea what kind of territory was below. I crossed my legs to keep from straddling a branch or wire, guarded my face with my hands, and waited.

Presently I saw the outline of the ground and a moment later was down in a cornfield. The corn was over my head and the chute was lying on top of the corn stalks. I hurriedly packed it and started down a corn row. The ground visibility was about one hundred yards.

In a few minutes I came to a stubble field and some wagon tracks, which I followed to a farmyard a quarter of a mile away. After reaching the farmyard, I noticed auto headlights and a spotlight playing over the roadside. Thinking that someone might have located the wreck of the plane, I walked over to the car. The occupants asked whether I had heard an airplane crash and it required some time to explain to them that I had been piloting the plane and yet was searching for it myself. I had to display the parachute as evidence before they were thoroughly convinced. The farmer was sure, as were most others within a three-mile radius, that the ship had just missed his house and crashed nearby. In fact, he could locate within a few rods the spot where he heard it hit the ground, and we spent an unsuccessful quarter of an hour hunting for the wreck in that vicinity before going to the farmhouse to arrange for a searching party and to telephone St. Louis and Chicago.

I had just put in the long-distance calls when the phone rang and we were notified that the plane had been found in a cornfield over two miles away.

It took several minutes to reach the site of the crash due to the necessity of slow driving through the fog, and a small crowd had already assembled when we arrived.

The plane was wound up in a ball-shaped mass. It had narrowly missed one farmhouse and had hooked its left wing in a grain shock a quarter of a mile beyond. The ship had landed on the left wing and wheel and had skidded along the ground for eighty yards, going through a fence before coming to rest on the edge of a corn field about a hundred yards short of a barn. The mail-pit was laid open and one sack of mail was on the ground. The mail, however, was uninjured.

The sheriff from Ottawa, Ill., arrived and we took the mail to the Ottawa Post Office to be entrained at 3:30 A.M. for Chicago.

A photomontage of the *Spirit of St. Louis* arriving in Paris.

CHAPTER THREE

Paris in the Spring

Within just a few years of Orville Wright's brief but historic 1903 flight off a North Carolina sand dune, daring aeronauts were knitting together odd corners of the map. In the summer of 1909, the Frenchman Louis Bleriot created a sensation by being the first to fly across the English Channel, a twenty-two-mile hop that was in its day as celebrated a long-distance feat as Apollo XI's round trip to the moon would become sixty years later. Bleriot, an unlikely hero whose navigational skills were so poor he almost missed England entirely, was greeted by a cheering crowd of 100,000 upon his return to Paris. The following month an enchanted public attended the world's first air show at Reims. That October, Count de Lambert concluded the latest in an unending string of long-distance flights—this one from Juvisy to Paris—by circling the Eiffel Tower in his Wright aeroplane.

The French, with their traditionally romantic self-image, were especially smitten with *les chevaliers de l'air*, making the cult of the poet-pilot an integral part of their national culture even as more than a hundred young French flyers died in the years between Bleriot's channel crossing and the outbreak of the First World War. Edmond Rostand captured the prevailing enthusiasm in his 1911 poem, "The Song of the Wing," claiming that powered flight was above all else *l'ame meme*—a spiritual undertaking.

As Charles Lindbergh and the industry both came of age together, flying machines continued to transport man ever higher, faster, and longer through the sky, creating excitement and adventure and opening up unlimited possibilities for their use. Technological progress was steady, with each new achievement building on the spectacular triumphs—and often fatal failures—of a swelling fraternity of tinkerers, mechanics, inventors, daredevils, and scientists. By the time Lindbergh learned to fly in 1922, airplanes were being catapulted off the decks of ships, used to "sky-write" advertising messages ten thousand feet above the earth, and journeying to some of the most isolated parts of the world. That year the *New York Times* illustrated an expedition to a remote part of New Guinea in a Sunday rotogravure section. Under the headline "Revered Messenger from the Skies," the *Times* reported: "The sensation caused to ignorant savages when for the first time they see an airplane sailing majestically through the skies and then gradually coming to the ground with its human freight can readily be imagined. At first consternation and then curiosity were evinced by the natives of Papua when the first airplane they had seen landed in the waters off their coast. They thought it was a god."

God, indeed. Flying was a deeply aesthetic experience, one that offered the potential for self-transendence and spiritual renewal. It seems almost quaint today, but in the early years of aviation there was a widespread mysticism attached to communing with the sky, a belief that something so rapturous would somehow develop into a benevolent instrument of social change. That nations co-opted flying machines for purposes of war was perhaps inevitable, but it did have the benefit of demonstrating aviation's practical side. Industrialist Henry Ford, for one, was involved in a variety of commercial ventures, including the development of a low-cost, single-passenger "flivver" plane that would provide the masses with a Model T for the sky; one day every home would come equipped with a garage and a hangar. Ford's son, Edsel, was interested in scientific applications, underwriting the polar flights of U.S. Navy Commander Richard Byrd. Byrd's headline-grabbing expeditions were only a sampling of the aerial adventures testing man and machine during the 1920s. Hardly a day went by when one didn't pick up a newspaper and read of some airman flying faster, farther, and at greater peril than the one before him. Throughout the decade, frontiers and records—along with a corresponding number of pilots and planes—fell with the regularity of autumn leaves.

In the fall of 1926, one major challenge loomed largest in the news: the conquest of the Atlantic. On the table was a $25,000 cash award offered by Raymond Orteig, a French-born New York hotelier who had created the Orteig Prize in 1919 as a way of strengthening the ties between his native and adopted countries. The money—and attendant glory—would go to the first to fly an airplane nonstop between New York and Paris in either direction, an epic journey of some 3,600 miles.

Actually, more than seventy people had already crossed the Atlantic in a variety of air machines, beginning with the five-man crew of the huge U.S. Navy flying boat that had lumbered 1,380 miles from Newfoundland to the Azores in May 1919. The seaplane, backed up by naval vessels deployed at fifty-mile intervals, made several emergency landings en route. One month later, Captain John Alcock and Lieutenant Arthur Whitten completed the first nonstop flight between the two continents, winning knighthoods and a hefty cash prize in the process. The British officers took off in a converted Vickers-Vimy bomber from St. John's, Newfoundland (the closest point in North America to Europe), and battled sleet, snow, and fog before crashing nose-first in an Irish bog 1,890 miles away. That same summer, a British dirigible carrying thirty-one crew members (and one stowaway) completed a round trip between the British Isles and Long Island. More transatlantic crossings occurred in 1924, one involving a German dirigible and the other a trio of Army planes following the usual Newfoundland-Greenland-Ireland path between the continents. But the limitations of existing aircraft still prevented pilots from making the much longer direct flight between New York and Paris.

Due to rapid improvements in aircraft design and technology, however, by 1926 such a flight was not only feasible, but likely to occur soon. New engines were now capable of lifting the weight of enough gasoline, at six pounds per gallon, to allow a plane to connect the two continents in a single bound. That year an American syndicate announced it was bankrolling the bid of Rene Fonck, France's top ace during the

Lindbergh was rebuffed in his attempt to buy the one existing Wright-Bellanca when its owner, Charles Levine (right), insisted that his company's pilot, Clarence Chamberlin (left), be at the controls for the transatlantic flight.

war, to capture the prize. Lindbergh, in St. Louis flying the mail, followed this first attempt with great interest.

In the early morning of September 21, 1926, Fonck was at the controls of his huge biplane, poised for takeoff at Long Island's Roosevelt Field. Designed by Russian aviation pioneer Igor Sikorsky, it featured three air-cooled radial engines that were more powerful and weighed less than standard water-cooled engines. Working against this advantage, however, was the payload, which included as many frills as necessities. The plane carried a convertible bed, two radio sets, flotation bags, and a crew of four. The seats were upholstered in red leather. Sikorsky had wanted time for more tests, but Fonck and his backers were eager to make the attempt before winter weather set in over the Atlantic. The fabled French élan, some suggested, would prevail. As if to underscore that belief, at the last moment a bag of croissants was brought on board. The pastries presumably would help tide the crew over until they got to Paris and could partake of the champagne and hot celebration dinner of Long Island duckling and roast turkey stored in the cabin.

Takeoff was like trying to coax an elephant into a high jump. The overloaded plane trundled down the runway and strained to get airborne, but its wheels never left the ground. It crashed through a fence at the end of the runway and dropped into a gulley. A split second later, the 2,830 gallons of fuel on board exploded into a fireball. Fonck and his copilot managed to escape the inferno, but the navigator and radio operator were incinerated.

The disaster was shared with millions via newspapers and newsreels, heightening interest in the Orteig Prize. Lindbergh analyzed the tragedy and came away convinced that he could succeed where the dashing Fonck had failed.

• • •

The Wright-Bellanca monoplane that Lindbergh coveted was a prototype designed by Giuseppe Bellanca specifically to showcase the nine-cylinder Wright "Whirlwind." The lightweight, air-cooled radial engine was built by the Wright Aeronautical Corporation in Paterson, New Jersey. It produced nearly 200 horsepower and averaged 9,000 miles between failures. Lindbergh focused his energies and pinned his hopes on buying the one-of-a-kind aircraft, which he felt certain could carry him safely across the Atlantic.

The first order of business was to find financing. He had $2,000 in a Detroit bank, but he needed several times that amount. As an occasional flight instructor, he had become acquainted with several of St. Louis's leading businessmen. This coalition of civic-minded aviation buffs (most were private pilots) wound up bankrolling his dream.

Earl C. Thompson, a wealthy insurance executive who owned his own plane, was the first to invest in Slim Lindbergh. Next were Major A. B. Lambert and his brother, Wooster. Harry Hall Knight, partner of a brokerage house and president of the local flying club, not only came on board, he introduced him to the influential Harold M. Bixby, head of the chamber of commerce. Bixby and Knight promised that they would help raise the funds needed for a Paris flight. Before too long Knight's father, Harry F. Knight; Lindbergh's boss, Major William Robertson; and E. Lansing Ray, owner of the *St. Louis Globe-Democrat*, had also pledged their support.

In late November, Charles took the train to New York for a round of meetings. Never a clothes horse and eternally thrifty, Lindbergh nonetheless spent $100 for a new suit, overcoat, scarf, and fedora. "I haven't the slightest use for them," he admitted. "I hate to do things just to make an impression. But right now that may be as essential to my Paris flight as a plane itself. . . ." He spoke with Bellanca, an Italian immigrant whose headquarters was his Brooklyn garage, and learned that it was the Wright Corporation, not Bellanca, who owned the plane. In a meeting with Wright executives, he was told that their prototype was in the process of being sold for $25,000, considerably more than the $8,500 Lindbergh's financial angels had raised. Keenly disappointed, Charles began exploring the idea of having a plane custom built for him.

In early February 1927, Charles received a surprising cable from Bellanca, informing him that he was now associated with a new enterprise called the Columbia Aircraft Corporation. The firm had acquired the Wright-Bellanca and would consider selling it to him. Lindbergh hurried to New York. There the young, impetuous millionaire owner of Columbia Aircraft, Charles Levine, said he could have the Wright-Bellanca for $15,000. Lindbergh returned to St. Louis to see if his backers would agree to the price. He explained that the aerodynamically advanced plane needed little more than to be fitted with fuel tanks and run through a few tests before tackling the Atlantic in the spring.

The syndicate quickly raised the money with a bank loan. "What would you think of naming it the *Spirit of St. Louis?*" asked Harold Bixby.

Charles thought it was a good name. In fact, he had earlier entertained the idea of a public subscription, asking the citizens of St. Louis to donate ten dollars apiece to buy a plane with their city's name emblazoned on its fuselage.

"All right," he agreed, "let's call it the *Spirit of St. Louis.*"

Lindbergh arrived at Levine's office in the Woolworth Building on February 19, 1927, a cashier's check for $15,000 in hand. He had a bombshell dropped on him. As a

As Lindbergh (identified by arrow) watches, the freshly fabricated wing of the *Spirit of St. Louis* is lifted by crane from the second story of the Ryan plant onto a boxcar before being lowered carefully to the ground.

condition of the sale, Levine insisted on being able to select the crew that would fly it to Paris. That probably would be Clarence Chamberlin and Bert Acosta, two top American pilots that he had recently hired. Lindbergh was speechless. Levine told him to call the following morning at eleven. When Charles did, Levine asked, "Well, have you changed your mind?" Lindbergh, livid, slammed the receiver down.

Time and money had been wasted pursuing the Wright-Bellanca. Lindbergh's spirits sagged. Several teams in the U.S. and Europe had already been formed to compete for the Orteig Prize; more were on the way. Most featured deep-pocketed sponsors and such well-known flyers as Chamberlin, Fonck, and Byrd.

Charles fell back on his plan of having a plane built to his specifications, though only one of the manufacturers he had contacted over the winter of 1926–27 had agreed to work with someone with his limited resources and lack of reputation. That was the Ryan Aircraft Corporation, a small, financially struggling firm headquartered in a nondescript building on the San Diego waterfront. At the end of February Lindbergh went to California to meet with president Franklin Mahoney and chief designer Don Hall. They came to terms on price and delivery time. For $10,580, Ryan would manufacture a plane capable of getting Lindbergh to Paris and deliver it within sixty days. It would be equipped with a Wright JC5 engine, a new and more powerful version of the Whirlwind, and the latest in instrumentation, including an earth inductor compass that would make it easier for Lindbergh to hold a course during the estimated thirty-six-hour flight.

Lindbergh was the first pilot to seriously consider making the flight alone in a single-engined plane. Many believed that a multiple-engined plane offered the best

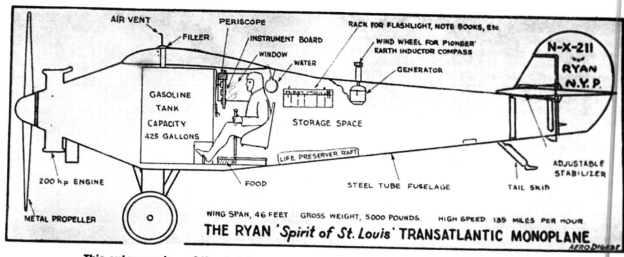

This cutaway view of the *Spirit of St. Louis* appeared in *Aero Digest*.

chance for crossing the Atlantic safely, but even in the case of single-engined craft the conventional wisdom was that there should be a second crew member. (Floyd Bennett, for example, had piloted Richard Byrd's flights while his more famous associate handled the charts, compass, and sextant.) In Lindbergh's view, the trimotored planes favored by several contenders only tripled the chances of engine failure; a hobbled aircraft might be able to land safely, but it would be unlikely to reach its final destination running on two engines. The idea of an expanded crew was predicated on the assumption that, even if one person could handle the twin chores of navigation and actually flying the craft, he could not possibly stay awake for the entire duration of the flight. Charles figured the risks of traveling alone were offset by the benefits: less weight, which meant increased range, and no worrying over the opinions or welfare of somebody else. As was often the case throughout his life, Lindbergh preferred going solo.

Lacking the time to develop an entirely new design, Hall created a strut-braced, high-winged monoplane out of two existing Ryan models, the Brougham and the M-2. The standard M-2 fuselage was extended 42 inches to produce an overall length of 27 feet, 8 inches, and the wingspan increased from 36 to 46 feet. Lindbergh chose to have the five oversized fuel tanks installed in front of the enclosed cockpit; in case of a crash, he wouldn't be crushed between the engine and the tanks. Hall pointed out that the unusual positioning cut off all forward vision. This didn't bother Charles, accustomed as he was to flying in the rear cockpit of his De Havilland. When he wanted to see what was ahead, he could bank the plane and look out either of the side windows. As a precaution, Ryan workers fashioned a periscope out of a tube of sheet metal and a pair of mirrors.

The tanks were designed to hold 425 gallons of gasoline. Assuming a cruising speed of roughly 90–95 miles per hour, with no help from a tail wind, this gave the plane a theoretical range of 4,100 miles—enough to reach Paris with a reserve of 500 miles. To squeeze every last mile out of the *Spirit*, Lindbergh eliminated all unnecessary weight. He decided against bringing along a radio (which he considered unreliable) and a parachute (which he thought impractical), saving a combined 110 pounds with those two items alone. He also trimmed the borders off maps, ripped pages out of

Lindbergh poses with a modified "Keep Out" sign in front of the hangar at Dutch Flats.

his notebook, had his seat made of wicker, even turned down a stamp collector's $1,000 offer to take a pound of mail to Paris—anything to save a few ounces. Although he had little faith that he would survive an emergency ditch into the ocean, he did allow for an inflatable raft, flares, Army rations, and an Armbrust cup, a device that could turn condensed moisture from his breath into drinking water.

Lindbergh's major concern was his navigation skills. He had rarely flown more than a few hundred miles nonstop, and never over water. Celestial navigation—steering by the moon and the stars—would be problematic. He knew that he'd be unable to hold a sextant steady enough to get an accurate reading of the longitude and latitude while simultaneously working the plane's controls. He would depend on dead reckoning; that is, determining his position from an hourly log showing the course flown, the distance made, and the estimated drift. He plotted his "great circle" course (the shortest distance between two points on the earth's curved surface) from New York to Paris in thirty-six separate segments. Each segment represented one hundred miles, or roughly one hour's flying time. "At each point I marked down the distance from New York and the magnetic course to the next change in angle," he explained.

Lindbergh always considered himself fortunate to have hooked up with Ryan. He liked Mahoney's enthusiasm, admired Hall's ability at the drafting table, and enjoyed the camaraderie of company workers. The firm wasn't going to make any money on this job, but with Ryan's reputation riding along with Lindbergh, employees willingly worked long hours of unpaid overtime to get the plane out on schedule. One of those workers was a young metal finisher named Douglas Corrigan, who eleven years later would become celebrated as "Wrong-Way" Corrigan for flying from New York to Ireland when his intended destination was Los Angeles. (Some would consider his misadventure a planned stunt and not a spectacular mistake.) It was Corrigan who, after 3,850 man-hours to design and build the *Spirit of St. Louis*, pulled the wheel chocks from the plane when Lindbergh took it for its first test flight on April 28. On the *Spirit's* wings was its government-mandated identification number: N-X 211. "N" was the international code letter for the United States, while "X" indicated that the plane was experimental. (The manufacturer had designated it the Ryan NYP, the initials standing for "New York to Paris.")

Charles put the *Spirit* through a week of speed and load tests at Dutch Flats outside San Diego, all the while half-expecting to hear at any moment that one of his rivals had successfully crossed the Atlantic. He had settled on a contingency plan should that happen: he would attempt a transpacific flight by way of the Hawaiian Islands, in many ways a riskier proposition.

But one by one, entrants were being eliminated or delayed. On April 16, Byrd's giant three-engined Fokker, *America*, crashed during a test flight in New Jersey. Of the four crew members, Floyd Bennett was the most seriously injured, suffering a crushed leg and punctured lung. Byrd broke his wrist. It would take time to mend men and plane.

A deadlier fate awaited the crew of the *American Legion*, a trimotored Keystone biplane that bore the name of the veterans organization that sponsored it. Ten days after the *America* crack-up, the *American Legion* sank into a swamp outside Langley Field in Virginia while on its final test flight. Lieutenant Commander Noel Davis and his navigator, Lieutenant Stanton Wooster, were unable to get out of the cabin and suffocated. That brought the number of airmen killed in pursuit of the Orteig Prize to four.

The toll would soon climb to six. In the early hours of May 8, as Lindbergh anxiously waited out a spell of bad weather in San Diego, two French war aces, Charles Nungesser and his one-eyed copilot, Francois Coli, took off from Le Bourget airfield near Paris, bound for New York. The fuselage of their stripped-down biplane, *L'oiseau blanc* ("The White Bird"), was designed to float once they made their planned splashdown in New York Harbor. Lindbergh, like many observers, felt sure these two experienced flyers would make it.

Nungesser and Coli never arrived at their destination. Although sightings were reported over Newfoundland and off the coasts of Nova Scotia and Maine, it became obvious by nightfall on May 9 that something had gone terribly wrong. Search parties were launched, but to this day no trace of the pilots or their plane has ever been found.

Newspapers were filled with speculation over the fate of the missing Frenchmen when Lindbergh finally left San Diego for St. Louis on the afternoon of May 10. His plan was to fly the last half of the 1,500-mile trip in darkness, giving him some prac-

Before leaving San Diego, Lindbergh gathered with a group of Ryan employees for an obligatory photograph touting Red Crown Aviation Gasoline.

tice in nighttime navigation, and then to continue on to New York. Despite encountering engine trouble over the Rockies, he landed in St. Louis with an excellent shot at establishing a new cross-country record. City fathers had organized a formal dedication and several ceremonies to welcome the *Spirit of St. Louis*, but Lindbergh's backers understood his urgency to get to New York as soon as possible. In lieu of the scheduled banquet, Charles grabbed some ham and eggs at his old Lambert Field hangout, Louie's Shack, then snatched a few hours' sleep before resuming his quest the following morning. He arrived at Curtiss Field on Long Island on the afternoon of May 11, having flown from coast to coast in an elapsed time of 21 hours, 45 minutes. He just missed mowing a path through the crowd of reporters and spectators that came running onto the landing strip, all clamoring for a closer look at this "brave Lochinvar out of the west," as one observer described him.

The sudden arrival of the previously unheralded Lindbergh and his odd-looking craft injected fresh excitement into what the *New York Times* was calling "the most spectacular air race ever." With the crash of the *American Legion* and the disappearance of *The White Bird*, the contenders now boiled down to Byrd, Chamberlin, and the dark horse the press dubbed the "Kid Flyer."

Byrd's *America* had been repaired and was undergoing tests at Roosevelt Field, adjacent to Curtiss Field. However, the odds-on favorite was Charles Levine's *Columbia*, if only the organization could get its act together. In Chamberlin and the *Columbia*, Levine had what most observers considered to be the best plane and the best pilot in the race, but his meddling got in the way. In early April, Chamberlin and Acosta

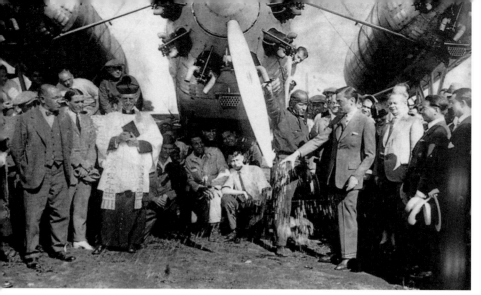

New York Mayor Jimmy Walker christened Rene Fonck's three-engined Sikorsky in September 1926, but the heavily loaded plane crashed on take-off, incinerating two crew members. Later, the famous French air ace stopped by to wish his competitor good luck.

Lindbergh and his mother at Curtiss Field on May 14, 1927.

had proved the Wright-Bellanca capable of crossing the Atlantic by setting a new endurance record of 51 hours, 11 minutes. After a minor crash pushed back the timetable for an ocean crossing, Levine had gotten cute in deciding who would actually fly the ship to Paris. He hired navigator Lloyd Bertaud to replace one of his pilots and announced at a press conference that a lottery held just before takeoff would determine whether Chamberlin or Acosta was left behind. This was too much for Acosta, who joined Byrd's team. To make the situation more bizarre, Chamberlin and Bertaud then filed separate legal actions against Levine over contractual matters, while designer Giuseppe Bellanca went to court seeking to regain majority control of Columbia Aircraft. As all this was taking place, the *Columbia* sat inside a locked hangar, unable to fly because of a court order. At one point the glory-grubbing Levine considered offering Lindbergh $25,000 to take him along as a passenger. "I will try to think of a place to put Mr. Levine," Charles laughed when Chamberlin told him of Levine's desperation.

The race was indefinitely put on hold the second week of May when the Atlantic was socked in by rain and fog. Deteriorating apace with the weather was Lindbergh's relationship with the media. Initially, he admitted, publicity was part of his overall plan to draw attention to his flight. "It would increase my personal influence and earning capacity. I found it exhilarating to see my name in print on the front pages of America's greatest newspapers, and I enjoyed reading the words of praise. . . ." He respected certain publications and their representatives, such as the *New York Times* and *Aero Digest*.

But the media quickly became a nuisance. Photographers tried to get him to pose with publicity-seeking actresses and once stormed into his hotel room, hoping to snap a picture of him in his pajamas. The reporters milling around his hangar or camped inside the lobby of the Garden City Hotel (where all the pilots stayed) fabricated quotes, invented or messed up details about his past, and pestered him with insipid questions. "Do you carry a rabbit's foot?" they asked. "Do you have a girlfriend? What's your favorite kind of pie?" Their simplistic stories often portrayed him as some kind of aw-shucks hayseed or death-defying stunt pilot (the "Flyin' Fool") instead of an experienced aviator who had soberly calculated his chances and was meticulously preparing for every contingency. On one occasion their antics on the airfield forced Lindbergh into making an awkward landing, causing him to damage the *Spirit*'s tail skid.

Worse, reporters had tracked down his mother and were harassing her at school and at home. They emphasized the dangerous aspects of his "suicidal" flight to the point that Evangline caught an overnight train to New York to have her suddenly magnified concerns smoothed over in person. Her impromptu visit was made to order for photographers, who asked the Lindberghs to hug for the cameras. They refused the syrupy pose; it was not their style to be publicly demonstrative. This didn't stop one tabloid from pasting their heads on a pair of surrogate bodies and publishing the bogus shot of loving mother embracing her devoted (and probably doomed) son.

• • •

On the evening of May 19, a wet Thursday in New York, Lindbergh was on his way to Manhattan to see a Broadway musical with several companions when one final per-

The early morning hours of Friday, May 20, 1927. As police line the runway, the *Spirit of St. Louis* is towed into position at Roosevelt Field.

functory phone call to the weather bureau produced a news flash: after seven days of bad weather, the front over the North Atlantic was lifting. With that Lindbergh hurried back to Long Island to get himself and the *Spirit of St. Louis* ready for takeoff at first light.

As Ryan's Franklin Mahoney supervised the *Spirit*'s preparation inside its floodlit Curtiss Field hangar, Lindbergh crossed to Roosevelt Field. He expected to find Byrd getting the *America* into shape for a dawn departure. To his surprise, Byrd—evidently influenced by the steady rain—was not around. There was no activity in the *Columbia* camp either, though Chamberlin was spotted in the hotel lobby, waiting anxiously for word that the injunction grounding the plane had been lifted. As the only experienced bad-weather pilot in the transatlantic derby, Lindbergh knew the downpour was inconsequential. What really mattered was what lay beyond this local system. And the weather updates continued to report clearing skies over the Atlantic.

Around midnight he returned to his hotel, hoping to catch at least a couple hours of desperately needed sleep. He posted a friend at his door with strict instructions to keep intruders out. Just as he was dozing off, the guard unaccountably walked into the room and asked, "Slim, what am I going to do when you're gone?" His sleep ruined, Lindbergh got dressed and returned to Curtiss Field at 3 A.M. There he helped with last-minute adjustments to the *Spirit of St. Louis*.

Success depended on the Wright engine performing flawlessly. This would be the most strenuous test yet for the Whirlwind, which "had to make 14,472,000 explosions perfectly and smoothly" during the planned thirty-six-hour flight, observed an engi-

It's approximately 7:35 A.M. on May 20, and Lindbergh gets some help putting on his flight suit (top photo). A couple of minutes later, he received best wishes and updated weather information from Commander Bryd (bottom) before climbing into the *Spirit of St. Louis.*

neer for Vacuum Oil, one of several companies to send a technical representative to assist Lindbergh. "Even a minor engine problem might bring a sudden and fatal end to a brave and thrilling adventure."

The "mirror girl," an elusive footnote to the Lindbergh story, appeared at this time. Part of the growing crowd gathered outside the roped-off hangar door, she overheard him discussing with mechanics the need for a small mirror to keep in view his new liquid magnetic compass. Because of the lack of space, the compass had been installed on top of the fuselage, inches above Lindbergh's head.

"It will give you a more accurate indication up there than any other place we can find," a mechanic said. "It will swing less in rough air. You sure haven't any extra room in here."

"I don't mind reading it through a mirror," replied Lindbergh. "The most important thing is to have it accurate and steady."

The men inside the hangar looked around for a suitably sized mirror. Then a "neatly dressed" woman, "not much more than college age," stepped forward, Lindbergh recalled.

"Will this do?" she asked, pulling a compact mirror out of her handbag. It was about two inches round. The size was perfect. It was stuck to the instrument panel, above the earth-inductor compass dial, with a wad of chewing gum. There it stayed, reflecting Charles'ss course all the way to Paris.

As a way of thanking her, the rope was lifted and she was given a look inside the cockpit. Lindbergh never learned her name and never saw her again. A quarter-century later, he was still wondering about her intentions. "Was she among the few who maintained unreasoned confidence in my success," he wrote in *The Spirit of St. Louis*, "or was hers a gesture of compassion toward a man about to die . . . ?" (Aviation historian Ev Cassagneres, having spent years chasing down the mirror girl's identity, is satisfied that the anonymous donor was a young brunette named Mrs. Loma Oliver, although everything else about her remains a mystery.)

The improvisational nature of Lindbergh's effort extended to his choice of sustenance for the long trip. Almost as an afterthought, he had brought along a sack of sandwiches: two ham, two beef, and one egg salad. A journalist, knowing the elaborate meals of the other pilots in the race, smiled at the meager fare. Charles defended himself. "If I get to Paris," he said, "I won't need any more, and if I don't get to Paris I won't need any more either."

Shortly after four o'clock the rain slackened and the *Spirit of St. Louis* was moved from its hangar to the runway at Roosevelt Field. Lindbergh was far from inspired by the sight of his plane, shrouded and dripping, being towed through the mist. He thought it looked "more like a funeral procession than the beginning of a flight to Paris."

Although the press had all along played up the notion of a great Atlantic air race, in reality the rival pilots—all of whom came to see Lindbergh off—were more cooperative than competitive. Byrd was especially charitable, offering updated weather information and the use of an elongated ramp, built at his own expense, at the east end of Roosevelt Field. Charles would have used it, but whatever wind there was was blowing in the wrong direction.

The *Spirit* was placed at the west end of the field and over the next three hours was slowly filled with 451 gallons of fuel. While the plane was being serviced, well-wishers tried to force on him a variety of good-luck charms, including a kitten, which many newspapers would mistakenly report had been taken along. But the only talisman he carried on the flight was a St. Christopher medal that a local woman, Katie Butler, had taken from around her neck and handed to a policeman to give to him. Lindbergh, his mind focused on more important matters, distractedly pocketed the gift. Many hours later over the Atlantic, he would be surprised by its presence inside his flying suit.

At 7:40 A.M., Charles shook hands with Byrd and climbed into the cockpit. Under his flight suit he was wearing a white shirt, knotted at the collar with a red-and-blue striped tie, a jacket, and Army breeches tucked into high boots. On his head was a wool-lined leather helmet; he also wore lined gloves and goggles to protect him from the elements. He carried a $500 bank draft, his passport, and several letters of introduction from Colonel Theodore Roosevelt Jr., whom he had met a few days earlier.

To Lindbergh, takeoff was the most dangerous part of the flight. He was at the controls of what was essentially a flying gas tank, or what the tabloids termed a "flying coffin." He faced problems beyond the sticky mud and lack of head winds. Mechanics had done everything they could think of to save weight, even replacing the grease in the wheels with lubricating oil. Nonetheless, the 2,750 pounds of gasoline boosted the overall weight of the plane to 5,250 pounds. This was over a thousand pounds more than the *Spirit of St. Louis* had ever carried before. To make the launch even more challenging, once Lindbergh started the engine he discovered the high humidity was causing it to turn at only 1,470 RPM. This was thirty revolutions lower than maximum capacity. Assuming he got airborne, would he have enough power to clear the telephone wires rising menacingly at the end of the runway?

All eyes were on Lindbergh. With the engine spluttering, he sat inside the thin walls of his cramped cabin and weighed the risks of trying to leave under less than ideal conditions against those of waiting an additional day. By then his rivals would likely be ready for departure as well. (Actually, the *Columbia* would remain grounded by legal problems for nearly two more weeks, while Byrd's chief financial supporter, department store magnate Rodman Wanamaker, wanted the *America* put through additional tests.) In this situation, with an underpowered engine trying to lift an overloaded aircraft off a sticky, unpaved runway, nobody would have faulted him for postponing his departure until the sun dried out the field and the air.

"It's less a decision of logic than of feeling," he later explained. "The kind of feeling that comes when you gauge the distance to be jumped between two stones across a brook." And if he had gauged wrong—well, that was the advantage of going it alone. He had no one to answer to except himself.

He buckled his safety belt and pulled down his goggles.

"What do you say," he said. "Let's try it."

With a nod from Lindbergh the wheel blocks were kicked out. A handful of men pushed against the wing struts to free the *Spirit* from the ooze, then ran alongside to help send the silver monoplane on its way. After a hundred yards the last of the helpers dropped away and the fishtailing plane was moving on its own, churning through the muck in the general direction of the ambulance parked ominously at the end of the runway.

This aerial view shows the muddy condition of Roosevelt Field as Lindbergh prepared to take off.

John Miller was a young aviation buff who had spent a sleepless night on the floor of the lobby of the Garden City Hotel, waiting for history to be made. "I think most of the non-aviation people out there expected a crash," he said of the hundreds of curiosity-seekers who had flocked to Roosevelt Field in the wee hours of a rainy morning. "They were out there to see a disaster."

The *Spirit* moved down the runway, the engine at full throttle, picking up speed and splashing through puddles. As it ate up more and more of the nearly mile-long strip, Lindbergh resisted the temptation to abort. He had earlier marked the spot on the runway where, if he felt that he had not gathered enough speed to lift off, he would throttle back and attempt to coast to a stop (the plane had no brakes), but now pilot and plane roared past the point of no return. The wheels bounced once . . . twice . . . three times . . . and then the *Spirit* finally became unglued from the earth, slowly rising above and then past the web of telephone wires. The barograph required by the National Aeronautic Association, installed a few hours earlier, began its official recording of time and altitude. It was 7:54 A.M., Friday, May 20, 1927.

A local youngster, Anne Condelli, had joined her parents and brother in seeing Lindbergh off. "There was a great relief," she told a documentarian many years later. "But there was no clapping, no joyful noises at all. Just relief that his plane had cleared those wires."

No photographs exist of the *Spirit of St. Louis* in flight over the Atlantic. Artist Mort Kuff conceptualized Lindbergh's utilization of ocean waves to aid his navigation. "During the entire flight," Lindbergh later wrote, "the wind was strong enough to produce white caps on the waves. When one of these formed, the foam would be blown off, showing the wind's direction and approximate velocity."

John Miller watched the plane disappear into the mist. He shook his head and said, "We'll probably never see the poor guy again."

• • •

Lindbergh flew along Long Island before pointing the *Spirit of St. Louis* across Long Island Sound toward Connecticut. Flying over this much water was a new and slightly unsettling experience. He knew that until gas consumption made the *Spirit* lighter, the fuel-laden plane was especially vulnerable to the waves of turbulence he was now encountering. He warily watched the wing tips bend with the strain of each new shock. However, a thousand feet over the Sound the choppy air suddenly turned calm. Pilot and plane settled down.

With his goggles pushed back on his head, Lindbergh filled out the first of his hourly logs, meticulously recording speed, altitude, visibility, wind velocity and direction, true course, and compass variation. He carefully noted oil temperaure and pressure, fuel pressure and mixture, and engine RPMs. Below the instrument panel was a complicated array of fourteen valves controlling the five fuel tanks. As he would do hourly throughout the flight, he switched tanks, manipulating the petcocks to ensure a balanced load. He hugged the New England coastline north, maintaining a steady speed of 105 miles per hour and an altitude of 200 feet, until reaching Plymouth, Massachusetts. There he headed out over the Atlantic. His next landmark, Nova Scotia, was more than two hours away.

This was the moment of truth—or supreme arrogance, as he later described it. Who was he, a pilot accustomed to using roads, railroad tracks, and other visible landmarks on the ground to guide him, to think that he could successfully navigate over such an immense and uninviting expanse of water and find, in succession, Nova Scotia, Newfoundland, Ireland, and Paris? Everything depended upon his having charted the great circle course correctly, and then using his compasses and the chart spread over his knees to make the necessary adjustments along the way. Lloyd's of London, which had been handicapping each entrant, certainly didn't think much of his chances. They refused to even post odds, believing the risk of one man flying a single-engined plane too great.

Charles flew a mere fifty feet above sea level from Massachusetts to Nova Scotia. In this age of uncrowded skies, a midair collision with another plane was highly unlikely, but he was careful to use his periscope to make sure there were no smokestacks or ships' masts in his path. He made St. Mary's Bay on the northwest end of the province and discovered to his satisfaction that after more than four hours of flying, he was only two degrees—six miles—off course. So far, his navigating had been solid.

During much of the next three hours, the time it took him to traverse the craggy Nova Scotia countryside, he had to contend with fog and heavy rain that forced him to make several detours. He emerged from the squalls still on course and slightly refreshed, the buffeting and the cold, wet weather momentarily reviving his dulled senses.

Fatigue was becoming as big a concern as bad weather. He had been without any real sleep for nearly thirty hours, with the lion's share of the flight still to come. Despite the chill, he decided against inserting the plastic windows he had brought along. He figured they would make the cockpit too warm, too cozy, too conducive to

The instrument panel of the *Spirit of St. Louis.*

a fatal sleep. He crossed Cape Breton Island in clear skies and headed toward New-foundland, two hundred miles distant.

During this first phase of his flight, his thoughts turned to his mother. "My mother, teaching school in Detroit—she's probably been at her laboratory desk all day, wondering and worrying, and trying unsuccessfully, with chemistry experiments, to curtain off in her mind a pilot and his plane. . . . I know what a message of my welfare would mean to her tonight." After a hectic day of dealing with antsy students and pry-ing reporters, Evangeline locked herself into the house she shared with her bachelor brother, Charles. She disconnected her phone and refused to see anybody. By the fol-lowing evening she would know whether her boy had made it or disappeared into the same black maw that had swallowed Nungesser and Coli.

It was perhaps with his mother in mind that Charles uncharacteristically veered ninety miles off course to buzz St. John's, the harbor town on the easternmost tip of Newfoundland. This would be his last contact with land before heading out over the ocean, the last human settlement for some 1,900 miles. He wanted people to see that he had made it this far. He knew that news of his sighting would be relayed over the radio; presumably word would reach his mother.

Charles checked his watch, which he kept set to Eastern Standard Time. It was a few minutes past 7 P.M. Friday, an hour behind local time. He had now covered more than eleven hundred miles in a little over eleven hours. Yet the most hazardous part of the flight was still in front of him: the "hop" across the frigid expanses of the North Atlantic to Ireland. The sun was setting over the horizon; blackness lay ahead and below. He plunged into the gathering darkness, a last few shards of light reflecting off the giant cakes of ice floating beneath him.

The *Spirit* hurtled through the moonless night. When Lindbergh raised its nose to 10,500 feet to climb over a towering fog bank and a developing storm, he suddenly found himself trapped inside a formation of ice clouds. "They're barbaric in their methods. They toss you in their inner turbulence, lash you with their hailstones, poison you with freezing mist. It would be a slow death, a death one would have long minutes to struggle against, trying blindly to regain control of an ice-crippled airplane, climbing, stalling, diving, whipping, always downward toward the sea." The wind tugged and pulled at the plane's fabric as if it were taffy. It was the most harrowing experience Charles had yet had inside the cockpit of the *Spirit of St. Louis*. But the craft held up under the buffeting and Lindbergh, drawing upon the bad-weather experience he'd gained from flying the mail, was finally able to manuever it into clear sky.

Because he was flying with the earth's rotation, Lindbergh actually spent only a couple of hours in total darkness. Entering his eighteenth hour of the flight, he had his spirits lifted by the sight of the moon rising to his left. What had heretofore been dark and formless regained dimension in the moon's pale light. He also passed the midpoint of his transoceanic crossing. As the *Spirit* raced towards the suffused light of the coming dawn, Ireland was now closer than Newfoundland. There was no turning back.

Meanwhile, Lindbergh did everything in his power to fight off the overpowering urge to nestle his head into a passing cloud and fall into a deep and immediate sleep. He stamped his feet, propped his eyelids open with his fingers, dove to within a few feet of the ocean's choppy surface to allow the cold spray to hit him in the face. He didn't eat anything for fear that a meal would relax him. Thankfully, the *Spirit* was a temperamental plane, requiring his constant attention to stay on course. Whenever he dozed off for even a second or two, he could feel it pulling away from him, and he would be jarred back to his senses. He flew on, dulled by fatigue and cramped muscles and repeating to himself that he had to stay awake or die. "Every cell of my being is on strike, sulking in protest, claiming that nothing, nothing in the world, could be worth such effort; that man's tissue was never made for such abuse."

Back in the states, suspense over the young flyer's progress carried through Friday evening and into Saturday. People who a few days earlier had never heard of Charles Lindbergh now tuned into radio bulletins and prayed for his safety. "I think half of America stayed home, glued to radios," said Elinor Guggenheimer, then a fifteen-year-old New Yorker. "You kind of held your breath: Where is he now? And what's happening? Can he possibly make it?" With no radio on board the *Spirit* and no sightings from the few ships out at sea, Lindbergh was as alone and incommunicado as any modern adventurer had ever been. "As Saturday dawned over the vast Atlantic," reporter George Hicks of WJZ radio told waking New Yorkers, "the Lindbergh plane is unreported since passing Newfoundland early last night."

Charles, unaware of the escalating public fascination with his flight, pressed on in his trancelike state. Over the next several hours, exhaustion and fog prevented him from taking accurate readings. Without making regular adjustments, it was possible that he had drifted hundreds of miles off course.

After more than a full day in the air, and two days without sleep, he was halfway

Lindbergh's destination: Le Bourget airfield outside Paris.

between sleep and consciousness, sharing an ethereal no man's land with a platoon of phantoms. As he later described it, the figures appeared "suddenly in the tail of the fuselage while I was flying through fog. I saw them clearly although my eyes were staring straight ahead. Transparent, mistlike, with semihuman form, they moved in and out of the fabric walls at will. One or two of them would come forward to converse with me and then rejoin the group behind."

The *Spirit* droned on. Then, during his twenty-sixth hour, he unaccountably emerged from his stupor. Something or somebody had given him a reprieve and he felt a sharpening of his senses. He spotted something below. It was a sea bird, a sign that he must be approaching land. Then occurred what he later called the most exciting moment of the entire flight: seeing several fishing boats rocking gently in the swells below. Surely a harbor could not be far off. But in which direction? He throttled back the engine and swooped down to within fifty feet of the water. As the *Spirit* glided like a big silver gull around one of the vessels, Lindbergh leaned out and shouted at the top of his lungs: "Which way is Ireland?"

There was no answer. He circled a second trawler, but the only response he got to his continued shouts was an expressionless face staring at him through a porthole. Several passes failed to bring anybody up on deck. Finally, seeing that he was wasting his two most precious commodities, fuel and daylight, he climbed away in disgust. It was now early Saturday afternoon. He had no way of knowing for sure how far off course he was. He headed east.

Before another hour had passed, Charles had the answer to his question. Which way was Ireland? It was directly in front of him, its welcoming presence signaled by high mountain walls and lush emerald fields. Sixteen hours after leaving the last landfall, Newfoundland, and two hours ahead of schedule (thanks to a healthy tailwind), he had reached Valentia and Dingle Bay on the southwest coast of Ireland. Villagers craned their necks in curiosity. Some waved. Charles was filled with emotion. It was like emerging from a long, dark tunnel. After spending a small eternity cut off from the mortal world and sharing the ride with phantoms, he was back among the living.

"Here are human beings," he gushed. "Here's a human welcome. Not a single detail is wrong. I've never seen such beauty before—fields so green, people so human, a village so attractive, mountains and rocks so mountainous and rocklike."

Equally heartening was finding that his dead reckoning had put him only three miles off course. Assuming no mechanical malfunctions, he could expect to be in Paris within another six hours.

Reports that Lindbergh had been sighted over Ireland began reaching America on Saturday morning. Premature shouts of celebration were outweighed by sober calls for cautious optimism. He still had to make England and then France, and anything could go wrong in terms of weather or equipment. Nonetheless, with every subsequent sighting of the *Spirit of St. Louis* the frenzy was cranked up a notch. People hung around newsstands, waiting for the latest extra edition, or bunched around radios, handicapping Lucky Lindy's chances between bulletins. The *New York Times* was inundated with 10,000 phone calls, while an emergency crew of switchboard operators at the *Detroit Free Press* were instructed to ask each caller, "Is this about Lindbergh?"

That morning's *New York Times* reported on the distracted fight crowd that had attended Friday evening's heavyweight bout between Jack Sharkey and Jim Maloney at Yankee Stadium. Before the bout, ring announcer Joe Humphreys had implored the crowd to "rise to your feet and think about a boy up there tonight who is carrying the hopes of all true-blooded Americans. Say a little prayer for Charles Lindbergh." Observed the *Times:* "Forty thousand persons put Lindbergh first and Sharkey and Maloney second. . . . The remarkable thing about last night's fight crowd was that they were all wondering how the transatlantic flight would come out and not who would be knocked out."

"Lindbergh Flies Alone," a piece written by Harold M. Anderson in the *New York Sun*, was already on its way to becoming the most widely reprinted editorial since Francis P. Church's "Yes, Virginia, There is a Santa" appeared in the paper thirty years earlier:

> Alone?
>
> Is he alone at whose right side rides Courage, with Skill within the cockpit and Faith upon the left? Does solitude surround the brave when Adventure leads the way and Ambition reads the dials? Is there no company with him for whom the air is cleft by Daring and the darkness is made light by Emprise?
>
> True, the fragile bodies of his fellows do not weigh down his plane; true, the fretful minds of weaker men are lacking from his crowded cabin; but as his airship keeps her course he holds communion with those rarer spirits that inspire to intrepidity and by their sustaining potency give strength to arm, resource to mind, content to soul.
>
> Alone? With what other companions would that man fly to whom the choice were given?

Alone, but carrying the hopes of millions, Lindbergh roared across the English Chan-

The Lone Eagle has landed! Pandemonium surrounds the *Spirit of St. Louis* at Le Bourget.

nel during his thirty-first hour, reaching the port city of Cherbourg just as the sun was setting over the French coast. Townspeople raised a cheer as the *Spirit of St. Louis* passed overhead.

Despite having been awake for more than two and a half days, sleep was no longer a concern. Euphoria had taken over. At 9:20 P.M. Charles unwrapped a sandwich, his first bite of food since leaving New York. It tasted stale, though, and he had to wash down each mouthful with a slug from his canteen. He balled up the wax paper and prepared to toss it out the window, then thought better of it. He didn't want to be an ugly American, littering the French countryside minutes into his first visit. To his pleasant surprise he saw beacons blinking dimly in the distance, marking the airway between London and Paris. Paris, sprawling and sparkling and little more than a half-hour away, would be impossible to miss. "From now on," he thought, "everything will be as simple as flying into Chicago on a clear night."

• • •

In Paris, news of Lindbergh's imminent arrival had spread throughout the city, causing a carnival atmosphere in the streets. A small army of newspapermen scrambled to cover what promised to be the biggest story since the war.

"Sometime in the afternoon the word came that Lindbergh had been sighted over Ireland," recalled Eric Hawkins, then a reporter with the English-language *Paris Herald*. "Immediately the French air and navy ministries alerted all Normandy and Channel ports to be on the lookout. Each new development sent fresh crowds of Parisians toward Le Bourget. The field was feebly lighted, but this was normal, and the runways were well marked. It was a fine clear night with a bright moon. A little after dark the word was flashed that Lindbergh had passed over Cherbourg, and from that moment on all of us knew he couldn't miss."

Lindbergh could not have been headed toward a more receptive people. Over the last several days there had been considerable gloom over the disappearance of Nungesser and Coli, and even some irrational grumblings that the United States had somehow engineered their fate. It had been suggested by some officials of both countries that, given the situation, any American attempt now would be regarded as being in poor taste. But the French could not help rooting for this unknown flying their way. *L'americain galant* embodied the essential elements of their own national self-image: valor, daring, élan. "Lindbergh deeply touched the French imagination," wrote Hawkins, "and despite the earlier failure of their own airmen Nungesser and Coli they desperately wanted him to succeed." It also didn't hurt the prickly French pride that he was flying a plane bearing the name of one of their greatest saints (as opposed to a craft called, say, the *Spirit of Little Falls*).

"In those days not every fourth Frenchman owned an automobile," Hawkins remembered. "Yet the road out through the northern gates of Paris in the direction of Le Bourget that Saturday at sunset must have carried most of the vehicles of the French capital then in operation. Added to these were taxis, some of Battle of the Marne vintage, buses and bicycles. And everywhere there were pedestrians, first in hundreds, then in thousands."

It was just a few minutes before ten o'clock when Charles spotted the Eiffel Tower and circled over, trying to get his bearings. Le Bourget lay thirteen miles northeast of the city. Despite being assured beforehand that it was a big airport and easy to find, he missed it on his first go-around and after several miles had to turn back. Looking out the window of the *Spirit*, he spotted a large black patch with a curiously irregular lighting pattern. One end was floodlit, while another was alive with crawling lights— car lamps, he finally determined.

Armand Deutsch, a young American from a well-to-do Chicago family, was lucky enough to be in Paris that long-ago spring evening. He had joined the throngs streaming towards Le Bourget, an impromptu welcoming committee that ultimately numbered some 150,000 people. Many had been merrily sharing bottles of wine for hours. They stood on the tops of cars, filled the roofs of airport buildings, and jostled each other behind the guarded fences separating them from the runway. As viewed from a thousand feet up in the sky, this massive assemblage was a dark, jellylike blob. Lindbergh had no idea what was awaiting him.

"Suddenly," recalled Deutsch, the moment still vivid after more than seventy years, "you could hear this small noise. And it grew a little louder . . . a little louder. And suddenly this small plane, caught in a shaft of light from the ground at Le Bourget, came into the view of all these people."

After several passes, the slightly puzzled Lindbergh decided that this probably was the right place and prepared for his final approach. As the crowd surged forward in rising excitement, Lindbergh executed a perfect sideslip landing on the dark end of the field. He taxied to a halt and tried to sort out his emotions. His euphoria was leavened with a certain sadness that the great adventure had actually come to an end. It was 10:24 P.M. (local time) on Saturday, May 21, 1927. He had flown nonstop 3,614

The headline of the *New York Times* says it all.

miles from New York to Paris in an official time of 33 hours, 30 minutes, and 30 seconds—and still had enough gas and stamina, he later insisted, to continue at least another thousand miles if he had wished. It was a shame to land, he reflected a quarter-century later, "with the night so clear and so much fuel in my tanks."

For now, though, he and the *Spirit of St. Louis* were going nowhere. In an almost frightening demonstration of unbridled adoration, Parisians exploded en masse past the barriers and guards and rushed towards the *Spirit* shouting "Lindbergh! Lindbergh! Lindbergh!" Many of the policemen joined the celebrants. The reaction of the crowd, said Deutsch, "was one of jubilation and disbelief, the likes of which I can't conceive of happening today about anything."

Charles cut the engine and sat helplessly inside his cockpit, tugging the cotton wool out of his ears. He had assumed that he would be quietly met by a handful of airport officials and reporters. "When I circled the aerodome it did not occur to me that

As thousands of Parisians cheer below in the streets, Lindbergh triumphantly waves American and French flags from the balcony of Ambassador Herrick's residence.

any connection existed between my arrival and the cars stalled in traffic on the roads," he confessed. "When my wheels touched earth, I had no way of knowing that tens of thousands of men and women were breaking down fences and flooding past guards."

This burst dam of humanity washed over Lindbergh and his plane. When he was finally able to speak, his first words were a simple, earnest query: "Are there any mechanics here?"

But the pandemonium—never mind the language barrier and the battering Lindbergh's eardrums had taken during the flight—made communication impossible. Clutching hands tore at him and the *Spirit*. In the turmoil someone made off with his flight log, a prize that has never been recovered. He was pulled from the plane and lifted onto the shoulders of the crowd, where he bobbed for several minutes before being rescued by some resourceful French fliers. One yanked off Charles's leather helmet and jammed it on the head of an American reporter, diverting the crowd's attention, while others threw a coat over his shoulders and hustled him off to safety inside a hangar.

In New York, Lowell Thomas informed his radio audience: "He made it! Charles A. Lindbergh, 'Lucky Lindy' as they call him, landed at Le Bourget airport, Paris, at 5:24 this afternoon." All across the country, factory whistles blew, church bells rang, car horns honked, and newsboys hawked special editions. Ball games, vaudeville shows, theatrical plays, and meals were interrupted in order to deliver word of his safe landing. Crowds formed on corners and in front of newspaper offices. Fire engines raced through streets, their sirens screaming. Orchestras struck up the "Marseillaise"

and "The Star-Spangled Banner." Some were moved to quiet reflection. "A young Minnesotan who seemed to have had nothing to do with his generation did a heroic thing," F. Scott Fitzgerald would write, "and for a moment people set down their glasses in country clubs and speakeasies and thought of their old best dreams."

• • •

Hours after being saved from the mob at Le Bourget, Charles was spirited away to the home of the American ambassador, a courtly old diplomat named Myron T. Herrick. There he ate a small meal of an egg and some bouillon, took a bath, spoke briefly to reporters, then went to bed for the first time in sixty-three hours, wearing a pair of borrowed pajamas. He woke early Sunday afternoon to find himself no longer an obscure air mail pilot from the Midwest. The bold-faced headline in the *Detroit Free Press* trumpeted his new status: LINDBERGH, IN PARIS, ACCLAIMED WORLD HERO.

The next few days were reduced to a head-spinning blur, as Charles was feted from one end of the City of Lights to the other. Parisians displayed American flags everywhere in his honor and launched cheers of "Vive Lindbergh! Vive l'Amerique!" in his presence. He won them over with his modesty, magnanimity, and simple grace, and grew in their esteem whenever he invoked the names of famous French aviators, which was often. On his first full day in France he requested a visit to the mother of Charles Nungesser. As thousands stood in the streets outside her apartment house, the weeping Mme. Nungesser kissed her visitor on both cheeks and praised him as a "very brave young man." She, too, had a brave son, she said, and she had not given up hope that he would be found alive. The next day Charles had his first taste of champagne as the Aero-Club of France awarded him its gold medal. He politely turned down the

Belgians examine the *Spirit of St. Louis*. "In your glory," King Albert told Lindbergh, "there is glory for all men."

A frenzied mob of 150,000 greeted the heroic American pilot in England. Lindbergh (in circle) was barely saved by an army of 1,200 whistle-blowing policemen, who hustled him through the melee to the control tower. There he addressed the crowd through a megaphone. "I just want to tell you this is worse than I had in Paris," he said.

Charles Nungesser (left) and Francois Coli in front of their Levasseur biplane, *The White Bird*, with its mocking death's head insignia. The two French war aces left Le Bourget for New York on May 8, 1927, and were never seen again.

accompanying gift of 150,000 francs, suggesting the money be used to help care for the families of French pilots who had died "for the progress of aviation."

It was one of the few times Charles said "no" while in Paris. Like the souvenir hunters who had partially dismantled the *Spirit of St. Louis* (now being repaired inside a guarded hangar), reporters, photographers, diplomats, and ordinary folks all wanted a piece of him. He obliged to the point of exhaustion, hurrying from one event to the next. "From the moment I woke in the morning to that when I fell asleep at night, every day was scheduled," he recalled. Parisians rioted to get closer to him. He was embarrassed when strangers insisted on kissing his hand, startled when women rushed up to peck him on the cheek, and humbled when Louis Bleriot, the father of French aviation, called him "the prophet of a new era." All the while, thousands of cables poured into the embassy, the congratulatory messages interleaved with a variety of fantastic commercial offers: $300,000 to appear in a motion picture for Paramount Studios, for example.

By Thursday, May 26, Parisians had still not tired of celebrating Lindbergh. That day an estimated one million of them turned out for a parade and reception. At City Hall, where he was seated like royalty in a golden chair, Charles received the key to the city and a specially designed gold medal. Early Saturday afternoon, following another full day of receptions and public duties, he fled the incessant festivities and feverish demonstrations the only way he knew how: by escaping in the *Spirit of St. Louis.* Before leaving his effusive hosts of the past week, Lindbergh circled the Eiffel Tower, performed several aerial acrobatics for the crowds gathered below, and dropped a weighted tricolored flag among them. Attached to it was a message: "Good-bye! Dear Paris. Ten thousand thanks for your kindness to me. Charles A. Lindbergh."

Lindbergh headed towards the airfield at Evere, Belgium, honoring a request to appear before King Albert and his queen, both enthusiastic pilots. With five thousand armed soldiers keeping a crowd ten times that number at bay, the greeting was considerably less raucous than the one he had experienced a week earlier at Le Bourget, but no less warm. Charles spent the weekend being feted at a series of private and public receptions, gathering a handful of decorations and awards in the process.

Then it was on to England. On Sunday, May 29, he crossed the English Channel and made for the Croydon Aerodome outside London. To his horror, the storied British reserve was nowhere to be found in the mob of 150,000 people swarming antlike over the field. Fearful of a disaster (he knew what happened when a person walked into a spinning propeller), he aborted his landing and circled the airport for several minutes while an overmatched army of bobbies tried to clear out a path. Upon his second touchdown the crushing mass of admirers damaged the *Spirit of St. Louis* and just barely missed getting to Lindbergh, who was snatched away in an automobile by members of the Royal Air Club. The chaos caused the official welcome to be canceled, but the balance of the next few days' festivities went on as planned.

A highlight was a private session with King George V. The king was fascinated with the practical aspects of the flight. "Now tell me, Captain Lindbergh," he asked at one point. "There is one thing I want to know. How did you pee?"

Charles explained that he had a hole in his wicker seat, which allowed him to urinate through a funnel into an aluminum container. He had disposed of the corked container somewhere over the French countryside.

The answer to another sensible question was taken out of his hands: Where to next, Captain Lindbergh? Charles had wanted to explore a bit more of the world. But America was calling—loudly and shrilly.

LINDBERGH, IN PARIS, ACCLAIMED WORLD HERO

ESTHER HANSEL SLATED AS CULT HEARING STAR

Testimony Expected to Outdo Previous House of David Revelations.

COURT TO TAKE RECESS EARLY IN COMING WEEK

Judge Feed Has Engagement Which Will Slightly Delay Trial.

BY JAMES P. POWERS
Free Press Staff Correspondent.

Benton Harbor, May 21.—With a cast of the state's chief critic of the House of David disclosing promotions gone by, a week that has been replete in sensationalism, the new attending narration is institutions, cupidity and abuses and others immorally and fraudulently by Benjamin, Mary and other leaders of the cult are in prospect.

(remaining column text not legible)

G. O. P. MEETING MAY COME HERE

Detroiters Hope to Land 1928 National Convention for This City.

(text not legible)

WORLD SPEED RECORD MADE BY SEAPLANE

Navy Flier Covers 130.93 Miles an Hour on Hampton Roads Course.

Washington, May 21.—(A. P.)—A new world speed record for seaplanes was claimed tonight by the navy for Lieutenant Rutledge Irvine, who was credited with a speed today of 130.93 miles an hour for 1,000 kilometers over the enclosed triangular course at Hampton Roads, Va.

FREE PRESS TODAY.

(index listing not legible)

SHOWERS ARE FORECAST FOR MONDAY, TUESDAY

DETROIT HAILS ITS "KID"

When Captain Charles A. Lindbergh made his successful landing in Paris, he was greeted with a message from the Detroit Board of Commerce:

"Detroit thankful for your safety. Heartiest congratulations."

(Signed)
Thomas S. Merrill—President Detroit Board of Commerce.
Harold H. Emmons—Chairman Aviation Committee.
Harvey J. Campbell—Secretary.

Another cablegram from Detroit was sent by the units of the 32nd Division National Guard:

"You exemplify the spirit of the National Guard in your marvelous achievement."

(Signed) Detroit Units, 32nd Division.

BULLETIN

St. Johns, Newfoundland, May 21.—(U.P.)—An unverified report reached here tonight that the missing French transatlantic fliers, Nungesser and Coli, had been picked up by a Grand Banks fishing schooner and brought to a south coast port. The report was entirely unconfirmed.

100-PASSENGER PLANES NEAR, FORD ASSERTS

Lindbergh Blazing Trail for Giant Commercial Ships, Detroiter Says.

(text not legible)

BATH BURIES 17 VICTIMS OF MAD MURDERER

Funeral Services for Twelve More Will Be Held on Sunday.

CROWDS STILL THRONG SCHOOL BLAST SCENE

Street Roped Off to Keep Bath Sightseers While Hearses Pass.

BY FRANK G. MORRIS
Free Press Special Correspondent.

Bath, Mich., May 21.—Stricken-eyed Bath writhed today as 17 small bodies were taken forever on an empty homes of this stricken community.

(remaining text not legible)

LOOMIS FACES TRIAL MONDAY

Judge Breman Denies Motion to Quash Information in Slaying Case.

(text not legible)

Auto Hits Trolley, Woman Is Killed

Miss Harriet Chandler, 58 years old, 6135 Ewald avenue, died in the receiving hospital yesterday as the result of injuries sustained May 17 when the automobile in which she was riding collided with a Baker street car at Chene and Baker streets.

Business Is Done In The Daytime

(text not legible)

Free Press Want Ads Produce Best Cost Less

DIVORCE DELAY INTERRUPTS HER WEDDING PLANS

MISS BELLE GREEN

The marriage of Miss Green, of Chicago, pending the ingenue lead to play in that city, to Fred C. Kraus, young business man of Detroit, has been delayed. Miss Green was to have been married on the day which this week came the play fact in the documents. It has not yet when the accident caused by her final decree of divorce, in charges of desertion, the waiting to be granted.

JOYOUS TEARS WET HER EYES; SON TRIUMPHS

Mrs. Lindbergh Weeps for First Time on Learning Boy Landed Safe.

'WHAT CAN I SAY BUT I'M HAPPY, GRATEFUL?'

Tired by Long Vigil, Mother Receives Flood of Congratulations.

BY CLIFFORD A. PREVOST

Le Bourget, France, May 21.—(U. P.)—Charles Lindbergh was too happy to speak for a few moments after arriving in Paris from New York. Tears streamed down the cheeks of the flying mail man. Finally he found his tongue.

"Somebody cable mother," he exclaimed. His mother lives in Detroit.

(remaining text not legible)

AIR HERO AND HIS MOTHER

MRS. EVANGELINE L. LINDBERGH AND HER SON IN FRONT OF HIS PLANE IN NEW YORK A WEEK AGO.

HE'S OUR BOY! DETROIT CRIES

City Celebrates Riotously Plans Grand Homecoming.

(text not legible)

FLIER'S LIFE LIKE FICTION

Public Had Come to Expect Much of Youth Before He Made "Hop."

New York, May 21.—(A. P.)—The life story of Charles Lindbergh, son of Mrs. Evangeline Lindbergh, Detroit teacher, is a record of the attainment of a high ideal held with unswerving determination.

(remaining text not legible)

LINDBERGH'S LOG

By United Press.

New York, May 21.—The list of previous trans-Atlantic flights is:

Friday, 7:51 a. m.—Captain Charles Lindbergh leaves Roosevelt field, New York, for Paris.

(remaining log not legible)

FIVE AIRSHIP FLIGHTS MADE PREVIOUSLY ACROSS OCEAN

New York, May 21.—The list of previous trans-Atlantic flights is:

May, 1919—American 3 seaplanes NC4 flew from Newfoundland to Lisbon, Portugal, stopping at the Azores.

June 14 and 15, 1919—Captain John Alcock and Lieut. Arthur W. Brown, British aviators, flew nonstop from St. John's, N. F., to Clifden, Ireland, 1,960 miles.

July, 1919—British airship R-34 flew from Scotland to New York and from New York to Pulham, England.

August, 1924—United States army round-the-world fliers crossed from Iceland to Greenland.

October 12-15, 1924—Zeppelin ZR-3, now the Los Angeles, was flown from Friedrichshafen, Germany, to Lakehurst, N. J.

AVIATOR DROPS TO SLEEP WHEN VICTORY'S WON

Lands Amid Cheering Thousands as New York-to-Paris Dash Is Completed.

MAKES EPOCHAL TRIP IN ONLY 33 1-2 HOURS

France Gives Rousing Welcome to Dauntless American, Who Wins $25,000 Prize.

By the Associated Press.

A new epoch in aviation has been inaugurated.

Charles Lindbergh, born in Detroit, landed at Le Bourget, France, at 5:21 p. m., eastern daylight time, (4:21 Detroit time), yesterday, in one record-smashing jump from Roosevelt field, New York.

"Well, here we are," was his greeting to the enthusiasm-maddened crowds.

Unaccompanied, Lindbergh drove his plane, "The Spirit of St. Louis," over the nearly 3,600 miles air track, clipping about two hours and a half off the most optimistic time allowance.

The world's imagination was fired by his exploit. Spontaneous celebrations in scores of cities both here and abroad lasted far into the night.

(remaining text not legible)

Lindbergh's Fame Brings Offers of Over $300,000

New York, May 21.—Rewards and opportunities for the youthful Charles Lindbergh who made aviation history today...

(remaining text not legible)

Ask Me Another

ON PAGE 13.

CHAPTER FOUR

Oh! What a
Wonder Boy Is He

Lindbergh's original plan to see a bit of Europe and possibly make a flight to the Orient went by the boards as America clamored for its Lone Eagle to return to his nest. Even his commander in chief, President Calvin Coolidge, had postponed his summer vacation in order to be in Washington for Charles's expected arrival. Lindbergh later jested that he had "found that it didn't make much difference whether I wanted to stay or not; and while I was informed that it was not necessarily an order to come back home, there was a battleship waiting for me." Actually, the U.S.S. *Memphis* that Coolidge dispatched to bring him home was a cruiser, but to judge by the way Lindbergh was being deified in the press, some idolaters saw no need for a vessel of any size. He could *walk* back across the Atlantic.

The *Memphis* arrived at Cherbourg, France on June 3, took on its acclaimed cargo (including the *Spirit of St. Louis*, carefully packed into two crates), and shoved off for the United States. While at sea, news came of a startling flight. Taking off from Roosevelt Field in the *Columbia*, Clarence Chamberlin and promoter Charles Levine, who had installed himself as copilot, had landed nearly two full days later in a cow pasture outside Eisleben, Germany, a trip of 3,905 miles that simultaneously broke Lindbergh's records for endurance and distance. A few weeks later, Commander Richard Byrd and three companions would narrowly complete yet another transatlantic crossing, the *America* crash landing in the water off the French coast. Each was an impressive and death-defying feat that not only contributed to the mushrooming public interest in aviation, but also demonstrated the quality of American airmen to the world. But while on each occasion the press whipped up the rhetoric to Lindbergh levels, neither Chamberlin's nor Byrd's aerial adventure excited the same kind of passionate response that Plucky Lindy's did.

For reasons that were not always that easy to articulate, Lindbergh's flight had captured the imagination like none other. Journalists, jitterbugs, and gewgaw makers all worked themselves into a lather. On the day he touched down in Paris the *New York Herald* alone sold an extra 114,000 copies, most readers agreeing with the *Herald*'s assessment of the flight as "the greatest feat of a solitary man in the records of the human race." At the Savoy Ballroom in Harlem, dance-happy patrons shouted

"Lindy's done it" and created a variation of the Charleston called the Lindy Hop. It became the dance craze of the nation. And the first wave of what would become a flood of Lindbergh-inspired merchandise, everything from sheet music to quickie biographies, rolled into stores.

While the city fathers of Washington, New York, St. Louis, and Detroit planned elaborate civic receptions, fantastic offers continued to pour in by cable. Motion picture contracts, book and lecture deals, vaudeville tours, product endorsements—all told, millions of dollars were waved under the young man's nose. Lindbergh, to whom the Wright Aeronautical Corporation had assigned the services of two public relations professionals, Dick Blythe and Harry Bruno, repeatedly said no.

The flyer's widely reported refusal to capitalize on his fame only added to his mystique. "Who *is* this Lindbergh?" wondered a country grown accustomed to the bald opportunism and vaporous notoriety of a succession of flagpole sitters and marathon dancers. The frenzy surrounding his return continued to mount. "You are in for it now," Blythe warned as the *Memphis* steamed closer to home. "You're the great American idol. Your time is no longer your own."

"I don't know about the idol part," Lindbergh responded. "But I do know I'm in a terrible mess."

The *Memphis*, accompanied by an escort of vessels and airships and awash in an ear-splitting stew of sirens, bells, whistles, cannonades, and cheers, docked at the Washington Navy Yard on June 11. It was a muggy Saturday in the nation's capitol. As high-ranking members of the government and the military waited respectfully but anxiously, Lindbergh enjoyed a private reunion with his mother aboard ship. Then the clean-cut wonder boy who had braved the Atlantic walked down the gangplank into his country's embrace. Life would never again be the same.

Hundreds of thousands of people lined the parade route while a record radio audience of 30 million people around the country listened to the proceedings. The procession that took Lindbergh to a specially constructed reception stand at the foot of the Washington Monument included a truck carrying 55,000 telegrams of congratulations; meanwhile, ten messenger boys struggled with a giant scroll that constituted a single telegram from Minneapolis bearing 17,500 signatures. President Coolidge delivered the opening remarks, making the already common allusions to Columbus, the Pilgrims, and Lindbergh's "Viking ancestors," after which the surprisingly verbose "Silent Cal" pinned the Distinguished Flying Cross on the guest of honor's lapel. The decoration had been specially created for Lindbergh, who also received a promotion to colonel in the reserves.

After several minutes of cheering, the object of all this adulation finally stepped to the microphone.

"On the evening of May 21," Lindbergh said in his clipped, high-pitched voice, "I arrived at Le Bourget, France. I was in Paris for one week, in Belgium for a day, and was in London and in England for several days. Everywhere I went, at every meeting I attended, I was requested to bring a message home to you. Always the message was the same.

" 'You have seen,' the message was, 'the affection of the people of France for the people of America demonstrated to you. When you return to America, take back that message to the people of the United States from the people of France and of Europe.'

"I thank you."

Unprepared for the brevity of the speech, the crowd waited a few seconds before bursting into applause. At 106 words, Charles showed that he could economize words as expertly as he rationed fuel. If nothing else, he needed to conserve his strength, for the whirlwind of private receptions and public ceremonies was just starting.

After a blurry succession of high-level banquets and medal-awarding ceremonies in Washington, it was on to New York for more of the same. On June 13, Lindbergh was transferred from a seaplane to a police launch to Mayor Jimmy Walker's yacht for final delivery to the southern tip of Manhattan. There were 300,000 people jammed into the Battery, but more than ten times that number were uptown, corraled behind police blockades or hanging out of windows.

The entire city had shut down for Lindbergh Day. Elinor Sullivan was one of the estimated four million people—which

Before leaving the cruiser *Memphis*, Lindbergh was presented with a model of the *Spirit of St. Louis*. The real *Spirit* had been carefully packed into crates.

amounted to two out of every three New Yorkers—who turned out in welcome. "The parade that went down Broadway, the people went wild," Sullivan recalled many years later. "They were throwing things out windows. Telephone books. Why half the people weren't hit in the head and killed, I don't know."

It took an hour for the procession, which included 10,000 soldiers and sailors, to crawl one mile up Broadway from Battery Park to City Hall. There robed trumpeters and grandstands holding 3,000 city officials awaited his arrival. "Colonel Lindbergh," said Mayor Walker, pinning an elaborately designed medal on his lapel, "New York City is yours. I don't give it to you. You won it."

The parade continued on Fifth Avenue. Along the way Lindbergh made stops to place a wreath on a monument honoring New York's war dead, to greet Cardinal Hayes in front of St. Patrick's Cathedral, and to periodically empty his car of the confetti that relentlessly rained down. It was the greatest blizzard to hit the city since the great snowstorm of 1888. The next day, an army of 2,000 whitewings had to sweep up a whopping 1,800 tons of paper, twelve times the amount that had accompanied the announcement of the armistice ending the First World War.

Lindbergh Day concluded with yet another medal ceremony in Central Park, this time Governor Al Smith draping the state's Medal of Valor—designed by Tiffany— around his neck, after which Charles and his mother retired to a Park Avenue apartment for some rest before leaving for a private banquet at the mansion of New York social lion Clarence Mackay, president of the Postal Telegraph Company. Several

Lindbergh addresses a crowd of 250,000 at the Washington Monument upon his return from France.

June 13, 1927: a blizzard on Broadway.

more days of receptions, both great and small, followed. The grandest was the official dinner of the City of New York at the Hotel Commodore, which at 3,700 guests was publicized as the largest banquet ever given an individual in the country's history.

That evening, former Supreme Court justice Charles Evans Hughes was his usual eloquent self. "We measure heroes as we do ships," he began, "by their displacement. Colonel Lindbergh has displaced everything."

His displacement is beyond all calculation. He fills our thoughts; he has displaced politics. . . .

For the time being, he has lifted us into the freer and upper air that is his home. He has displaced everything that is petty; that is sordid, that is vulgar. What is money in the presence of Charles A. Lindbergh?

What is the pleasure of the idler in the presence of this supreme victor of intelligence and industry? He has driven the sensation mongers out of the temples of our thought. He has kindled anew the fires of the eight ancient altars of that temple. Where are the stories of crime, of divorce, of the triangles that are never equilateral? For the moment we have forgotten. This is the happiest day, the happiest day of all days for America, and as one mind she is now intent upon the noblest and the best. America is picturing to herself youth with the highest aims, with courage unsurpassed; science victorious. Last and not least, motherhood, with her loveliest crown.

We may have brought peoples together. This flight may have been the messenger of good will, upon the character of those who cherish it. . . . Our boys and girls have before them a stirring, inspiring vision of real manhood. What a wonderful thing it is to live in a time when science and character join hands to lift up humanity with a vision of its own dignity.

There is again revealed to us, with a startling suddenness, the inexhaustible resources of our national wealth. From an unspoiled home, with traditions of industry, of frugality and honor, steps swiftly into our gaze this young man, showing us the unmeasured treasures in our minds of American character.

America is fortunate in her heroes; her soul feeds upon their deeds; her imagination revels in their achievements. There are those who would rob them of something of their lustre, but no one can debunk Lindbergh, for there is no bunk about him. He represents to us, fellow Americans, all that we wish—a young American at his best.

On June 16, Brooklyn celebrated its own Charles Lindbergh Day, with nearly three-quarters of a million people lining the twenty-two-mile parade route. Afterwards, a brief ceremony was held inside the Hotel Breevort, where an ornate check for $25,000 passed hands from Raymond Orteig to Lindbergh. Then it was off to another reception, another dinner, and another party, the latter featuring the mayor, Charlie Chaplin, and publisher William Randolph Hearst. Everybody, it seemed, wanted to meet the fellow that Cardinal Hayes had greeted as the "finest American boy of the day."

• • •

Preferring to be known as nothing more than a first-rate pilot who, through skill and

A NEW YORK WELCOME

This group of previously unpublished snapshots, taken by one of Lindbergh's Detroit relatives, captures just a portion of the hysteria that took place on June 13, 1927, Lindbergh Day in New York. "Colonel Lindbergh," said Mayor Jimmy Walker, "New York City is yours. I don't give it to you. You won it."

Part of the armada of more than 400 vessels that greeted Lindbergh upon his arrival in New York.

Lindbergh transferred from the seaplane *San Francisco* (background) to a police launch, which whisked him to the yacht *Macom* for special delivery to Manhattan.

Sailors march up Broadway.

Policeman strain to hold back some of the estimated 4 million people that lined the parade route.

Young ladies atop a float with a model of the *Spirit of St. Louis.* In front of St. Patrick's Cathedral, Cardinal Hayes of New York rose from his chair and greeted Lindbergh as "the first and finest American boy of the day."

diligent preparation, had accomplished one of the great feats in aviation, Colonel Charles A. Lindbergh was to his eternal dismay transfigured into that newest of modern creatures: a celebrity. Thanks to advances in newsreels, radio, photojournalism, and other instruments of mass communication during the 1920s, that insidious accompaniment of fame cynically known as "ballyhoo" reached a level never seen before and rarely matched since. If image wasn't quite yet everything in 1927, the expansion of the cult of personality—fueled by the growing and converging fields of advertising, public relations, and media—was nonetheless well underway in American life. In no time at all Lindbergh the hero was overshadowed by Lindbergh the celebrity; the fact that he was such big news made him even more newsworthy. His fame grew exponentially with the overwhelming media coverage of all of the subsequent pseudo-events: parades, banquets, medal ceremonies. Even the normally staid *New York Times* devoted its first sixteen pages to coverage of his Manhattan reception. The level-headed Lindbergh realized the absurdity of a fame that fed on itself. "I was so filled up with this hero guff," he told Dick Blythe after they left New York for yet another round of celebrations in St. Louis, "I was ready to shout murder."

Despite his protestations, in looks and demeanor Lindbergh was made to order for his assigned role of public hero. He was young, movie-star handsome, modest almost to a fault, and obviously considered his mother his best gal. (Lots of women were trying to change that, as evidenced by the 10,000 marriage proposals he received. In St. Louis, a group of starry-eyed ladies engaged in a free-for-all over the half-eaten cob of corn he left on his plate.) He was remarkably photogenic. An estimated 7.4 million feet of newsreel film was shot of him by the time the last flakes of confetti had fallen in New York. Meanwhile, newspaper and magazine photographers took thousands upon thousands of pictures of him. Whenever a camera caught him frowning, editors charitably labeled the expression of displeasure "Lindbergh's flying face." Nothing could tarnish the young man's image. "Colonel Lindbergh is a messenger from God," insisted the St. Louis man who offered to guard Lindbergh's growing pile of gifts and trophies for free.

Within a few months of his flight Charles received an astonishing three million letters, cables, and parcels. "Fair-haired Apollo," began one flowery missive, "your meteoric traverse of the sea, your transcendent victory over boundless space, shall thunder down the avenue of time!" Not since George Washington had an American been so universally and fulsomely praised. Those newspapers not comparing him

Philanthropist and aviator Harry Guggenheim convinced Lindbergh to embark on a three-month tour of all forty-eight states.

Lindbergh speaking at Springfield, Vermont, in July 1927, in one of the eighty-two stops he made on his tour.

to the father of the country (who, like Lindbergh, was "first in the hearts of his countrymen") or a Norse god trotted out analogies to more obscure historical figures, such as Louis IX of France. Wrote the *Baltimore Sun*: "Between the man who fared forth alone, defying the dark dreads of space . . . and the crusading king who fared forth from the glory and grandeur of the Court of France, under the Cross, daring the terror that awaited in heathen places . . . surely there is a spiritual bond that recks not of the intervening centuries or of the differences in racial origin."

Lindbergh was embarrassed by the comparisons. He was no emperor, certainly no god, but in his admirable unpretentiousness he attracted perhaps even more acolytes than if he had been. "The stiff military bearing of the others, that touch of dramatic superiority which can suggest so much in the air of a military victor, was totally lacking in Lindbergh," wrote Fitzhugh Green, covering the Washington welcome for the *New York Times*. "His hair was mussed; his stance awkward. But it was a mussiness and an awkwardness that made men cheer and women weep to see. . . ." Green noted that one radio broadcaster, affected by Lindbergh's unexpected genuineness, cried unashamedly on the air at the conclusion of his speech.

Journalists, intellectuals, and social commentators were almost desperate to analyze his fame and to understand the mania to which they were all contributing. "The popularity of Lindbergh is due to the fact that he has chosen to achieve an aim the whole world can understand and admire," opined the *New York Times*. "Every era has its allotted evangel. . . . Our faith is locomotion . . . To fly is thus a supreme mysticism. To fly across an ocean is the beatific vision. Charles A. Lindbergh is our Elijah." Lindbergh "has shown us that we are not rotten to the core," May B. Mullett wrote hopefully in *American* magazine, "but morally sound and sweet and good."

In Cincinnati, Lindbergh donned a bonnet and was made a member of the *Ku-ni-eh*, a Boy Scout honor society.

In 1931, Frederick Lewis Allen, the Harvard-educated associate editor of *Harper's Magazine*, examined the Lindbergh phenomenon in his book *Only Yesterday*. Despite occasional lapses of myopia, it remains a splendid social history of America during the 1920s. In Allen's view, once the hysteria surrounding Lindbergh's transatlantic crossing was stripped away, what remained was a "stunt flight" having "little practical advantage." After all, seventy-eight people had previously crossed the ocean by air (though none, of course, had done it alone). "Why, then," he asked rhetorically, "this idolization of Lindbergh?"

The explanation is simple. A disillusioned nation fed on cheap heroics and scandal and crime was revolting against the low estimate of human nature which it had allowed itself to entertain. For years the American people had been spiritually starved. They had seen their early ideals and illusions and hopes one by one worn away by the corrosive influence of events and ideas—by the disappointing aftermath of the war, by scientific doctrines and psychological theories which undermined their religion and ridiculed their sentimental notions, by the spectacle of graft in politics and crime on the city streets, and finally by their recent newspaper diet of smut and murder. Romance, chivalry, and self-dedication had been debunked; the heroes of history had been shown to have feet of clay, and the saints of history had been revealed as people with queer complexes. There was the god of business to worship—but a suspicion lingered that he was made of brass. Ballyhoo had given the public contemporary heroes to bow down before—but these contemporary heroes, with their fat profits from moving-picture con-

Dearborn, Michigan, had the distinction of building the first school named after Lindbergh. Work on the $120,000 elementary school began in late 1927 and was completed in time for classes to begin in September 1928. The dedication on October 9, 1929, featured remarks by Lindbergh's mother, a Detroit schoolteacher who had recently been awarded a Motherhood Medal by the Detroit Board of Education. "I think only one thing is greater than education," she said, "and that is motherhood."

Lindbergh's good-will tour took him to Los Angeles on September 20. There he received a gold loving cup engraved with the signatures of 36 movie stars. He also met several of them personally, including (from left) Douglas Fairbanks," America's Sweetheart" Mary Pickford, and Marion Davies, the mistress of publisher William Randolph Hearst.

babies, bridges—even railroad cars and a viaduct—were named after him. So were a town in southeastern Wyoming, a lake in Montana, and a mountain peak in Colorado. By year's end the publishers of *Time* magazine had created the "Man of the Year" award specifically for him and the newest of several schools bearing the Lindbergh name was under construction in Dearborn, Michigan.

The new year found him in the midst of a second good-will tour. It had started in mid-December with a record 27-hour nonstop flight between Washington and Mexico City, then continued on through fifteen Latin American countries. Upon his return in early 1928, he retired the *Spirit of St. Louis* to the Smithsonian Institution and received the Congressional Medal of Honor from President Coolidge. It marked the first time the nation's highest decoration for bravery had been awarded to a civilian.

Beginning on December 28, 1927, Lindbergh embarked on a self-financed two-month tour of Latin America. Here the *Spirit of St. Louis* has just landed at *Campo Lindbergh* in Panama, one of sixteen countries the "Ambassador of the Air" visited.

An unintended consequence of this high-profile globetrotting was to keep throwing logs on the fire of Lindy mania. His flying ambassadorship kept him in the news daily and more than doubled the number of gifts and decorations that flowed in after his Paris flight. The trophies, loving cups, proclamations, keys, portraits, honorary degrees, testimonials, resolutions, certificates of membership, addresses of welcome, bound scrapbooks, medals, stamps, busts, and good luck charms of every type joined the tennis racket from an admirer in Corona, New York, the plane made of tobacco from a fan in Kentucky, and the collection of flies ("Flies for a Flyer") from the Bug House of America in Butte, Montana. In all, Lindbergh received more than 15,000 presents from 69 countries. With no place to store this eclectic collection (then conservatively estimated to be worth about $2 million), he eventually donated it to the Missouri Historical Society.

As was the case with all of Lindbergh's attributes, his altruism grew to near mythic proportions. One of many examples was his change of heart over the $500,000 contract he had signed with William Randolph Hearst to star in a movie about aviation. Arguing Hearst's motives with his new friend and advisor, Harry Guggenheim, he had come to the conclusion that Hearst was more interested in using the film as a vehicle to promote the career of his mistress, actress Marion Davies. At Lindbergh's request, Hearst tore up the agreement. The media mogul was impressed enough to send the reluctant actor a pair of priceless 17th-century silver globes—one celestial, the other terrestial—that Charles had admired inside Hearst's New York apartment. They were among the items donated to the Missouri Historical Society.

On April 30, 1928, the disassembled *Spirit of St. Louis* was delivered to the Smithsonian Institution, where it has been on permanent exhibition ever since.

On December 13, 1928, four days before the twenty-fifth anniversary of the Wright Brothers' first flight, Lindbergh was photographed in Washington with the surviving member of the famous duo, Orville Wright. "How impossible it had been for Wilbur and Orville, on those sand dunes of North Carolina in 1903, to envisage the changes even a single generation ahead," Lindbergh later reflected.

As this particular episode demonstrated, Lindbergh truly did care first and foremost about furthering the cause of aviation, so in that sense money was always a secondary consideration. Still, a man had to make a living.

According to publicity agent Harry Bruno, Lindbergh was "never averse to cashing in on his flight. Once he realized how everyone was reacting to it, and to him, he resolved a plan to make it solve his financial problems, and made sure that he was never short of a dollar again. But that doesn't mean to say that he gave us carte blanche to endorse anything in his name. Just the opposite. He kept a tight hold on everything we were doing for him, and made sure that the only recommendations he made were for articles or projects directly associated with his flight or his interests. But for those we were to ask as much as the market would bear."

Charles endorsed only those products that he either used or genuinely believed in, such as Champion spark plugs, Vacuum motor oil, Waterman fountain pens, and the timepiece he wore during his flight ("Col. Lindbergh says: 'My BULOVA Watch keeps accurate time and is a beauty' "). He accepted a high-powered Franklin touring car, his first automobile, and posed in ads with the car and the *Spirit of St. Louis*. The pairing of Lindbergh and his plane was a natural one, for the two had become inseparable in the public mind. The marriage was reinforced by his habit of using the pronoun "we" when speaking of his flight. Charles actually was referring to his syndicate of St. Louis backers, but most Americans didn't know or care enough to make that distinction.

To Lindbergh's disappointment, *"We"* became the title of the book that was hurriedly produced in the period between the end of his New York homecoming and the start of his national good-will tour. The manuscript, which had been contracted with New York publisher George Putnam before the Paris flight, originally was ghostwritten in a first-person format by *Times* reporter Carlisle MacDonald—a common literary device that nonetheless struck Lindbergh as being mildly deceptive. Contributing to the author's dissatisfaction was MacDonald's bombastic style, so unlike his own. As Lindbergh went line by line through the finished manuscript, he finally determined that the book, if it was to carry his byline, needed to be almost completely rewritten. So, as Putnam and bookstores nervously waited, Charles holed himself up in Guggenheim's mansion and wrote 40,000 words of straight-forward prose in three weeks. The book was rushed to the printer and was in the hands of eager readers by the middle of July.

It was an instant best seller. At the end of its first month in print *We* had sold nearly 200,000 copies. It went through scores of editions, was published in several languages, and within a year earned its author roughly $250,000 in royalties. Lindbergh's bank account swelled with his book proceeds and the various money awards and syndication fees he collected: $50,000 from the Guggenheim Fund for his national tour, for example, and another $50,000 from the *New York Times* for the exclusive rights to the story of his Latin American tour. Various endorsements brought him between $10,000 and $25,000 apiece. These were not inconsiderable sums. New York Yankees first baseman Lou Gehrig, for example, made $7,500 in 1927.

Lindbergh's personal worth quickly grew with the salaries and stock options he received as chief consultant to two airline companies. By the onset of the Great Depression, less than three years after his flight to Paris, the once financially strapped air mail pilot would be close to being a millionaire—at a time when the term still meant something. If Lindbergh had not courted his enormous fame, he indeed capitalized on it. Unlike less dignified members of America's celebrity culture, however, the Lone Eagle had not feathered his nest with nearly as many dollar bills as he could have. It was one reason a fickle public did not sour on him as the decade of ballyhoo drew to a close.

In this cartoon the humor magazine *Life* spoke to Lindbergh's enduring popularity. For once, "ballyhoo" had staying power.

MALCOLM BINGAY

"*She smiled at my discomfiture*"

Longtime Detroit journalist Malcolm Bingay normally wasn't intimidated by the people he covered in the news. However, as this passage from his 1946 autobiography, *Detroit Is My Own Home Town* illustrates, he had rarely encountered the likes of Evangeline Land Lindbergh and her equally formidable son.

While I have never met the father, I have met his mother. You get some understanding of the cool and aloof Lindbergh after you have met her. She comes from one of the oldest families of Detroit—the Lands. Her uncle, John C. Lodge, was Mayor of Detroit when the boy was flying the ocean.

Legend has it that Lindbergh first came to Detroit to see if he could get his uncle, as mayor, to interest local aviation in financing his flight. Uncle John, as the story goes, chided the boy for risking his life in aviation, assured him there was no future in it, and urged him to settle down and get "a good steady job."

His mother teaches chemistry at Cass Technical High School. She returned to Detroit after the death of her husband. When the flight started I was managing editor of the *News*. I arranged to have a wire run out to her bungalow home on the east side, so that she could be kept informed on every flash that came in. My idea was that we would get a break on any comment she might make—*if* he landed.

When the news came in that he had made it, she was seemingly the only one in the world not thrilled.

"Thank you," she said. "That is all I want to know."

Later she did give the *News* a little more comment but not much. She barred herself to all reporters. The following morning she called her class together as usual at Cass Tech. They burst out in a wild ovation.

"Thank you, ladies and gentlemen," she responded crisply. "And now let us get on with our lessons."

I began looking up this curious lady. I found from James O. Murfin and others who were classmates of hers at the University of Michigan that it was generally agreed she was the most beautiful coed on campus. And a brilliant student. But serene and aloof to all the adoring young men who sought her companionship. Local society anticipated a big social wedding with one of our gay young blades and was startled when she met and married the grim lawyer from Minnesota with his passionate crusading for liberal causes.

Newspapers, maga-zines, and syndicates rushed representatives here to get her story on her son. She would see none of them. I was authorized by one of the syndicates to offer her $25,000 for ten articles on Lindbergh's boyhood. No answer at all. I appealed to Mayor Lodge.

"You do not know the little lady as I do," laughed the mayor. "All I can do is to make an effort to have you meet her and do your own arguing."

After days of delay she finally consented to see me in the mayor's office—after school.

She appeared as a lovely slim symphony in brown—a mite of a person compared with her six-foot-four son. Lodge introduced us.

"Permit me to thank you," she said in a soft musical voice, "for extending that wire to my residence when Charles was flying. But please do not get any idea that I am not fully aware of your purpose in so doing."

Malcolm Bingay

August 10, 1927: Mother and son are feted in a parade through downtown Detroit.

"I am authorized," I said, "to ask you if you will write a series of stories about your son—"

"I am not a writer."

"But we will hire any one of the best women writers in the country to act as your amanuensis."

"Whatever credit there is in this thing belongs to Charles. I do not propose to project myself into any ephemeral spotlight and bask in the reflection of his glory. I want you to understand—I am very proud of him. He achieved what he wanted to do. But what would you newspaper people have said if he had failed and been lost in the Atlantic?"

She had me stopped there because I had often thought the same thing myself.

"You owe something to the country," I started feebly. "After all, we must consider the inspiration your son's action will be to all young Americans. The story of his life—"

"Nonsense! If the world proclaims his glory I will not cheapen it by any such action on my part."

"Wouldn't $25,000 interest you?"

"Not $25,000,000! Have you no understanding of what I am driving at? Money does not mean that much to me."

I started to say something else when she waved a daintily gloved hand and turned to Mayor Lodge.

"Uncle John," she said, "will you please tell this gentleman the interview is over."

She smiled at my discomfiture. I had spoken so enthusiastically about her boy and pretended a desire to meet him.

"For being so nice about this," she said with a laugh, "when Charles comes to Detroit, I'll have you meet him."

I forgot all about that. But when he did arrive in Detroit on his triumphant tour, Mrs. Lindbergh called me on the phone. It had not been an empty promise. "If you will be at our suite at the Book-Cadillac at five o'clock I will arrange to have you meet Charles—as I told you I would," she said.

The guards would not let me in, but she came out to get me. That was the first time I met the "Lone Eagle." His greeting was about as warm as that which might exude from a frozen turnip. After several efforts to get a conversation started, I said to him:

"I want to congratulate you, Colonel, on having a wonderful mother."

"I know it," he said coldly.

I walked out.

When Henry Ford said one day that I ought to meet Lindbergh, that he was a most delightful fellow, I disagreed with some heat. But, later, when [publisher] John S. Knight and I were shown through the huge [Willow Run bomber] plant by Ford, I met Lindbergh for the second time. I have never been so agreeably surprised. Personality and charm, plus. As delightful a conversationalist as I have ever met.

A strange world, isn't it?

Charles and Anne Morrow Lindbergh, 1929.

CHAPTER FIVE

First Couple of the Sky

The *Spirit of St. Louis* pulled along flocks of Lindy wannabes in its slipstream. Applications for pilots' licenses tripled in 1927, the number of licensed aircraft quadrupled, airport construction boomed, and the public investment in aviation stock reached nearly $1 billion before Wall Street crashed. "Since Lindbergh's flight," marveled the editor of one trade magazine, "everything that happens in aviation appears to the public to be extraordinary." Another journalist ruefully noted the growing number of stunt pilots interested solely in instant celebrity. The flight to Paris "brought about a boom in aviation, to be sure, but a not altogether healthy one, and it led many a flyer to hop off blindly for foreign shores in emulation of Lindbergh and be drowned."

The baldest, yet most successful attempt to capitalize on Lindbergh's runaway fame was stage-managed by none other than his publisher, George Putnam. Even as copies of "*We*" continued to sell briskly in the spring of 1928, the master promoter arranged for a twenty-nine-year-old social worker named Amelia Earhart to accompany two male pilots in the *Friendship* in the latest attempt to hop the Atlantic. The novelty of a female crew member was much bigger news than the ocean crossing itself. Earhart's slim, boyish figure, short-cropped hair, blue eyes, and flashing white teeth reminded everybody of another photogenic transatlantic flyer. She was dubbed "Lady Lindy" by the press, as Putnam knew she would be. The trimotor Fokker took off from Newfoundland on June 17, 1928, and landed safely in Wales the following day, making the terrified passenger the first female to cross the ocean. This, as anticipated, immediately transformed her into a very marketable commodity. A book, a lecture tour, honors, endorsements, and job offers followed. (So did marriage, as Earhart succumbed to Putnam's Svengali-like charms.) New York threw the obligatory ticker-tape parade and gave her a key to the city.

Earhart, a capable pilot not yet qualified to fly multi-engine planes, felt more embarrassment than accomplishment. To her credit, history's most famous piece of luggage did something about it. On May 21–22, 1932, she became the first female to solo the Atlantic, piloting her Lockheed Vega from Newfoundland to Ireland in record time. That this Putnam production occurred on the fifth anniversary of Charles's Paris flight was no accident.

Earhart (who set a number of other speed and altitude records before disappearing over the Pacific in 1937) had already registered her feelings about her derivative nickname. "The title was given me, I believe, probably because one of us wasn't a

A 1926 photograph of the Morrow family. In the back row are (from left) Dwight W. Morrow, his wife Betty, and their daughters Elisabeth and Anne. Seated in front are the youngest children, Dwight Jr. and Constance.

swarthy runt. You understand my dislike of the title isn't because I don't appreciate being compared to one who has capabilities such as Colonel Lindbergh has, but because that comparison is quite unjustified."

Earhart wrote that letter in 1928 to a young woman she had recently met in the company of Colonel Lindbergh. Unlike the breezy and worldly Earhart, Miss Anne Spencer Morrow was shy and bookish and had led an insulated life. But soon the entire world would know the elfin brunette as the *real* Lady Lindy.

• • •

Charles first caught a glimpse of his future wife when he was invited to the New Jersey home of Dwight Whitney Morrow not long after his return from Paris. He was briefly introduced to the three Morrow girls—Constance, Elisabeth, and Anne—but evidently none made any impression on him.

This nonchalance toward the opposite sex puzzled gossip columnists, who regularly played matchmaker for America's most eligible bachelor. Lacking any cooperation from Lindbergh in this area, they reported on imaginary dates and mused over potential sweethearts. For his part, Charles was examining affairs of the heart in his usual pragmatic way. "A girl should come from a healthy family, of course," he observed. "My experience in breeding animals on our farm had taught me the importance of good heredity." Despite the unlimited opportunities for casual sex with all types of beautiful women, he would remain a virgin until he married.

Lindbergh established a rapport with Dwight Morrow, a short, rumpled-looking man who had risen from obscure West Virginia roots to a position of wealth and influence. Morrow was a graduate of Amherst and the law school of Columbia University and by 1914 was a partner in the banking house of J. P. Morgan. During the First World War he served as an adviser on transportation problems to General John J. Pershing and also helped arrange financial aid to the Allied countries. After the war, he helped get Cuba's finances back in order. In 1925, President Calvin Coolidge, an Amherst classmate, appointed him president of the Aircraft Board, which set national aviation policy. At the time Morrow met Lindbergh, he had just been appointed ambassador to Mexico, a post he would hold for three years. During his time away from the states, Morrow had a magnificent estate commensurate with his position and

tom Lockheed Sirius monoplane. Zipping along at 190 miles per hour at altitudes reaching 14,000 feet, and stopping only to refuel in Wichita, Kansas, the flying Lindberghs shaved nearly three hours off the existing speed record. During the entire 14 hours, 45 minutes, and 32 seconds they were in the air, Anne gamely weathered noise, vibration, and noxious fumes while performing her duties as co-pilot. A huge crowd awaited their arrival at Long Island's Roosevelt Field. When the plane landed, Anne—nauseated and near collapse—was hustled out of sight of cameramen and reporters. To Charles's indignation, some papers reported that she had suffered a nervous breakdown. A few days later, word got out that she was several months pregnant, news that the

Anne with baby Charles, born on June 22, 1930— her twenty-fourth birthday.

public found more electrifying than their flight. The press staked out Next Day Hill in anticipation of the blessed event, further rankling Charles.

On June 22, 1930, Anne's twenty-fourth birthday, the Lindberghs celebrated the arrival of their first child, a boy that they named Charles Augustus Jr. "When I first saw it," Anne confessed in a letter to her mother-in-law, "I thought, 'Oh dear, it's going to look like me—dark hair and a nose all over its face.' But then I discovered what I think is Charles's mouth, and the unmistakable cleft in the chin! So I went to sleep quite happy."

Because the Lindberghs were the closest thing the country had to royalty, the media treated the event as if it were the birth of a prince. However, Charles's awkward handling of the birth announcement irked many in the press. Still irritated over the "contemptible" newspapers that had dared write about Anne's condition, he released a photograph of the baby only to media outlets he considered "constructive." The offending papers easily obtained prints of their own, and for good measure fired a few shots at Lindbergh. This round of negative press reflected the first faint signs of disenchantment with the Lindbergh legend. With ordinary Americans lurching through the first year of the Depression, more than one thirty-dollar-a-week reporter began wondering just what it was that made the Lindberghs so special.

Charles had been under siege for years, a situation that he rued but that he had more or less learned to cope with. Now, with a family and hard times entered into the equation, he felt less secure than ever. Letters that used to ask for an autograph or a picture of the Colonel now asked for money. Some *demanded* it, threatening harm if they didn't get any.

While many of his fellow citizens lived from day to day, Charles's finances were

Juan C. Trippe, the legendary head of Pan American Airways, hired Lindbergh as his technical adviser in 1929.

sound and his future guaranteed. He was the chief technical adviser of Transcontinental Air Transport (known after its incorporation of Western Air as TWA) and Juan C. Trippe's Pan American Airways. Each airline paid him $10,000 a year in salary. Far more lucrative were the stock options he received. TAT, which called itself "The Lindbergh Line" in its advertising, gave him 25,000 shares at ten dollars a share; the stock quadrupled in value after he joined the organization. He cashed out his premium shares in both companies for $400,000 while still retaining good-sized blocks of stock. He also benefitted from being a Morrow son-in-law; in effect, he had married into the House of Morgan. He was put on the bank's preferred list. This allowed him to buy blue-chip stocks at a steep discount and then sell them at the market price for a substantial profit. In addition, Anne entered the marriage with a trust fund of $500,000. To help put these numbers in perspective, know that in 1930 a person could buy a round-trip plane ticket between New York and Los Angeles for $160, a new Chevrolet roadster for $495, and a tailored suit (with two pairs of pants) for $40.

Charles moved in circles that would have shocked his father. He found himself at dinner parties and inside smoking rooms with the likes of millionaire John D. Rockefeller Jr. (who thought the young man "remarkably mature in his judgments") and politician Herbert Hoover (whom he publicly endorsed for president during the 1928 campaign). C. A. Lindbergh had spent most of his adult life thundering against the cozy clique of moneyed interests that influenced national policy-making. Now his son was married to the daughter of a banker-politician whose estate needed thirty servants to keep it running smoothly.

Not everybody in the silk-stocking set was enchanted with the Lone Eagle. Some privately felt that, if not for the Paris flight, he probably would be running a gas station on the outskirts of St. Louis. There were occasional lapses of decorum to back up their judgment. At a dinner party in 1930, for example, Charles poured mouthwash into a decanter of rare Burgundy wine—a practical joke that one of the guests, columnist Dorothy Thompson, considered "atrocious." He also had the less than genteel habits of blowing his nose without a handkerchief and spitting. Nonetheless, many

The *Spirit of St. Louis* wings its way towards France, as depicted by artist Terry Lundby.

An ornate check for $25,000 passed hands from Raymond Orteig to Charles Lindbergh on the evening of June 16, 1927. In accepting the Orteig Prize at New York's Hotel Breevort, Lindbergh said, "I do not believe any such challenge, within reason, will ever go unanswered."

Countless medals were struck in commemoration of Lindbergh's flight, including this one by the Paris Mint.

Although hastily written, Lindbergh's account of his Paris flight was a national best-seller. *"We"* went through scores of editions and netted its author six-figure royalties.

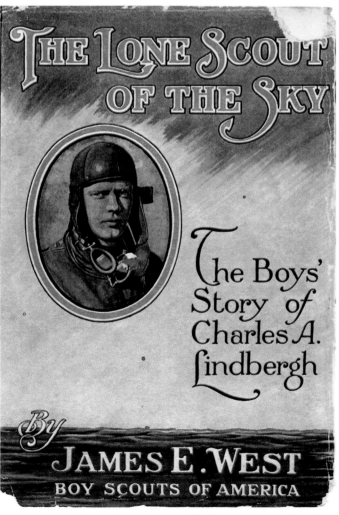

One of the earliest biographies of Lindbergh was written by James E. West, the Chief Scout Executive of the Boy Scouts of America.

America's greatest hero rides up New York's Broadway through a storm of confetti on June 13, 1927.

Atlant-flygaren Charles Lindbergh.

Charles Lindbergh
der Oceanflieger

Lindbergh's fame knew no borders. In Sweden he was known as the *Atlant-flygaren* and in Germany as *der Oceanflieger*. In England, the firm of Lambert & Butler included him in their 50-card set of "The World of Sport" cigarette cards.

NEW YORK 7:51 A.M. MAY 20TH   PARIS 5:21 P.M. MAY 21ST

CAPTAIN CHARLES "PLUCKY" LINDBERGH

NEW YORK · TO · PARIS · IN · 33½ · PARIS · N.Y.

LINDBERGH "SPIRIT OF ST. LOUIS"

A sampling of the numerous badges and pins inspired by Lindbergh's Paris flight and his subsequent good-will tour of the United States.

OUR INTERNATIONAL HERO

Souvenir Program

Lindbergh Day

FARGO
AERONAUTICS
CLUB

FARGO, NORTH DAKOTA
AUGUST 26,
1927

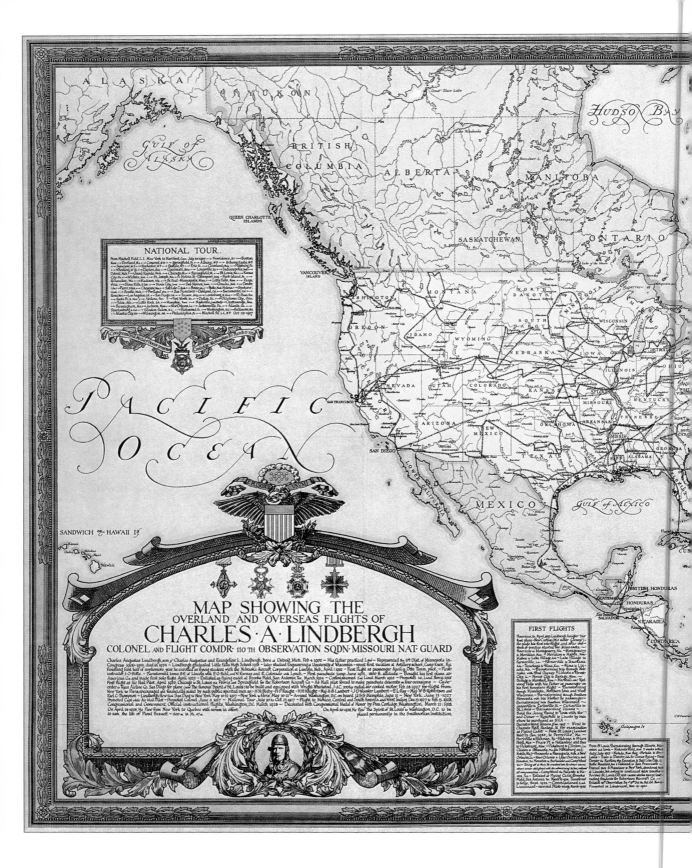

MAP SHOWING THE
OVERLAND AND OVERSEAS FLIGHTS OF
CHARLES·A·LINDBERGH
COLONEL AND FLIGHT COMDR· 110 TH OBSERVATION SQDN· MISSOURI NAT· GUARD

A map showing Lindbergh's 1927–1928 flights in the *Spirit of St. Louis*.

Three board games inspired by Lindbergh and the *Spirit of St. Louis*. There were many others.

A wide variety of Lindbergh merchandise flooded the marketplace in the late 1920s, including the items found on this page: a razor, bookends, a commemorative plate, and Lucky Lindy cigars.

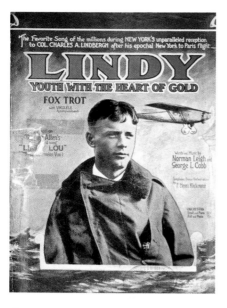

Some 300 songs were written about Charles Lindbergh, including marches, waltzes, hymns, and fox trots. The majority were published between 1927 and 1936 and covered the key events of his life: the Paris flight, his marriage to Anne Morrow, their trip to the Orient, the birth of their first child, the baby's kidnapping and murder, and, finally, the execution of Bruno Richard Hauptmann.

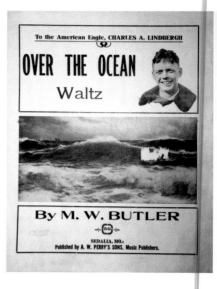

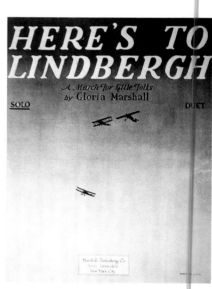

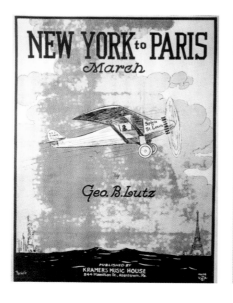

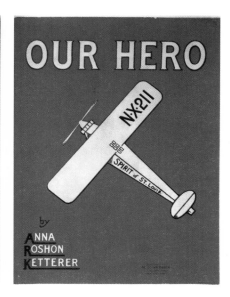

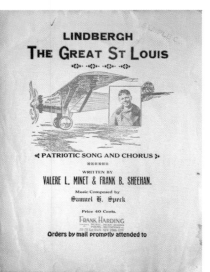

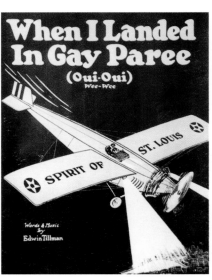

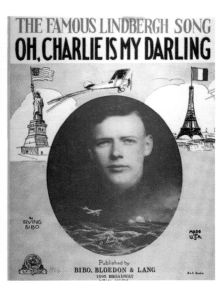

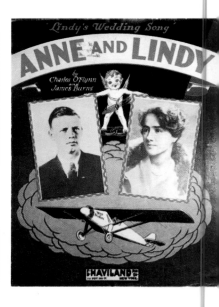

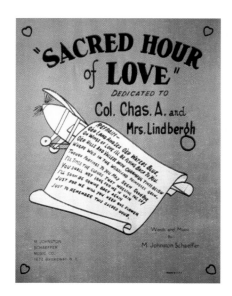

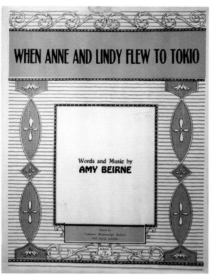

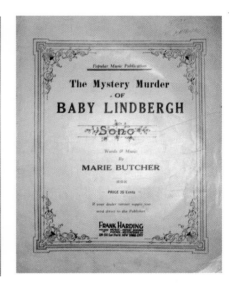

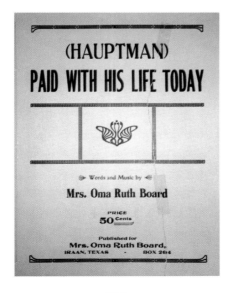

American Creed

I Believe in the United States of America as a government of the people, by the people, for the people; whose just powers are derived from the consent of the governed; a democracy in a republic; a sovereign nation of many sovereign states; a perfect union, one and inseparable, established upon those principles of freedom, equality, justice, and humanity for which American patriots sacrificed their lives and fortunes. I therefore believe it is my duty to my country to love it; to support its constitution, to obey its laws; to respect its flag; and to defend it against All Enemies.

Left: This "American Creed" featuring Lindbergh was sold by veterans during the 1930s. On it Lindbergh (who did not endorse the card) pledged to defend his country "against All Enemies," a promise he kept after his isolationist views became moot with the Japanese bombing of Pearl Harbor.

Below: "Lindbergh's Secret" by Rhode Island artist Domenic DeNardo depicts Lindbergh (second from left) piloting a P-38 on the morning of June 27, 1944, during his first of several combat missions with the 475th Fighter Group. Rounding out the formation are Major Thomas McGuire, Colonel Charles MacDonald, and Lieutenant Colonel Meryl Smith.

members of society's upper crust—initially drawn to Charles by his celebrity—found themselves permanently attracted to his qualities. Among those was Colonel Henry C. Breckinridge, a tall, refined Wall Street attorney who had been assistant secretary of war under Woodrow Wilson. Breckinridge became a close friend and his longtime legal advisor. Another was Harry Guggenheim, whose Long Island mansion had a bedroom suite kept exclusively for Charles's overnight stays.

For all his wealthy and well-connected friends, Charles was anything but a social climber. He was always most comfortable around those with grease under their fingernails, be they pilots, mechanics, or tinkerers. Learning of Robert Goddard's experiments in the nascent field of liquid-fueled rockets, he took it upon himself to find patrons for the "moon-mad" physicist's underfinanced research. By 1930, thanks to Lindbergh's unflagging support, Goddard had set up a laboratory and testing range in Roswell, New Mexico. Goddard died in 1945, and, although much of his work was underappreciated in his lifetime, he laid the scientific foundation for space exploration. In 1969, as Apollo XI astronauts prepared to touch down on the lunar surface, the *New York Times* formally retracted a 1920 editorial that had belittled Goddard's claim that rockets would one day break free of earth's gravity and fly to the moon.

Charles cultivated a much deeper relationship with Dr. Alexis Carrel, a man who was nearly thirty years older but treated him like a peer. The controversial Nobel Prize-winning biologist was on the staff at the prestigious Rockefeller Institute for Medical

Lindbergh also was technical adviser to Transcontinental Air Transport, which later changed its name to Trans World Airlines. For years TWA was known as "The Lindbergh Line." In this photo, Lindbergh sits in the cockpit of the *City of Los Angeles*, the Ford trimotor that launched transcontinental service between New York and Los Angeles in 1929.

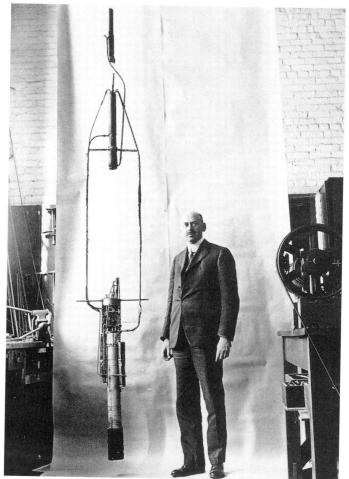

Physicist and rocket pioneer Robert Goddard in 1925, standing next to the world's first liquid-propellant missile. Lindbergh was one of the first to appreciate and champion Goddard's research.

Research in New York. The two men, giants in their respective fields, were introduced by a mutual acquaintance in 1930. A pioneer in the areas of vascular surgery and artificial transplants, the French-born Carrel alienated many of his associates with his short temper, large ego, and eccentricities. His operating room was painted completely black and he insisted that his assistants wear black uniforms and hoods during surgery. He dabbled in mysticism. According to Lindbergh, Carrel "believed in the supernatural realm. He was always searching for bridges between the physical and the mystical. He studied developments in the new field of psychosomatic medicine, listened intently to accounts of mental telepathy and clairvoyance, and was convinced of the efficacy of prayer."

Carrel's experimental research fascinated Charles. He was interested in finding a way of keeping tissues and organs alive in vitro; that is, in an artificial environment outside of the body. He kept a sliver of heart muscle from a chicken embryo growing inside a flask for twenty years, an event that was celebrated annually by Carrel and staff members singing "Happy Birthday" to the cultured tissue. For the rest of the decade, Charles would spend much of his free time with Carrel at the institute. Carrel, "a man overflowing with ideas and philosophical concepts," would greatly influence Charles's thinking on all sorts of matters.

Charles lacked formal scientific training, but he was able to make excellent use of his mechanical aptitude and analytical skills in the laboratory. His most significant contribution was inventing an ingeniously designed machine that he called a "perfusion pump" and the *New York Times* described as an "artificial heart," thus coining a term. "The Lindbergh invention worked this way," science writer Christopher Hallowell explained on the fiftieth anniversary of the pump's 1935 unveiling, "an organ from a freshly killed animal—usually a fowl or a cat that had been bled to death—was placed in the main chamber, and a glass tube fitted to its main artery. The chamber was then sealed, and the machine, placed in an incubator, was activated. Air hissed through tubes and into the rotating valve, whose concavities forced gas to flow

The Lindberghs inside their Lockheed Sirius seaplane on July 27, 1931, at the beginning of their trailblazing trip to the Orient.

into the glass apparatus in alternating pulses, pushing artificial blood up from the base of the machine into the organ. After flowing through it, the fluid drained out by gravity and fell into a pressure-equalization chamber before returning to the lower reservoir for recycling. . . . Organs had been kept alive on it for up to twenty-one days; there was no reason, Carrel and Lindbergh said, why they could not be sustained indefinitely."

Although the pump was not a direct predecessor of the artificial hearts developed in the 1980s by Dr. Robert K. Jarvis and Dr. William Pierce, it "was an inspiration that showed that life could be sustained by a machine that works very much like the heart," concluded Hallowell. In its time Lindbergh's perfusion pump was acclaimed as a sensational scientific advance, an achievement, many thought, that was on a par with the creator's flight across the Atlantic. The accolades did not surprise Anne, who wrote that the pump was "not a fluke, not chance, not charm and youth and simplicity and boyishness, but the expression of a great mind."

• • •

In the summer of 1931, following months of planning and with little Charlie barely a year old, America's "first couple of the sky" embarked on a great-circle survey flight to the Far East. This was a remarkable expedition. In a ten-week voyage that took them through the northernmost fringes of the world, Charles and Anne proved the shortest route to the Orient was through Alaska. In the process of mapping the route they became the first aviators to fly from America to China.

The Sirius had been equipped with a more powerful engine and fitted with pontoons, allowing Charles to splash down in lakes, rivers, and harbors. Once again, Anne competently served as navigator and radio operator and uncomplainingly shared in the hardships, though the press, as always, gave her little credit for the expedition's success. Because she didn't fly alone and abhorred self-promotion, Anne never was fully accepted into that exclusive sorority of top aviatrices that included Amelia

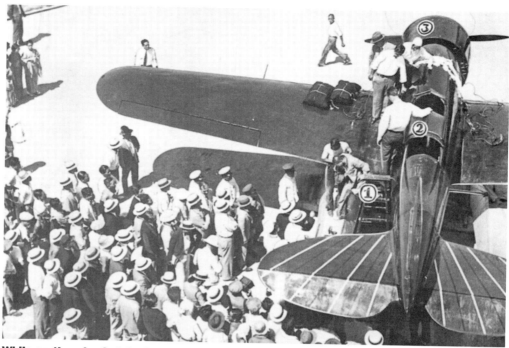

While on the wharf at Osaka, Japan, Lindbergh (number 2 in photo) discovered a young stowaway (number 1) huddled in the baggage compartment of the Sirius. "Life was not very happy at home," Anne (number 3) wrote later. "He had read in the newspapers about this aviator who had come from America—and would presumably go back there. Here was his chance to escape. He would go to America. Ironically enough, we were headed toward China."

Earhart, Louise Thaden, and Jacqueline Cochran. She did, however, create literature that put her on a par with the best poet-pilots of the era, including her idol, Antoine de Saint-Exupery. Beginning in the early 1930s and continuing for nearly a half-century, she would publish more than a dozen finely crafted volumes of nonfiction, fiction, and memoirs, as well as many essays, articles, and poems, making her one of the country's most widely read writers.

The 1931 flight formed the basis of Anne's first book, *North to the Orient.* The following passage describes the Lindberghs' anxiety in trying to find a place to land in the wilds of Alaska before dark overtakes them. In it can be found what the *Saturday Review of Literature* praised as the author's "seeing eye and singing heart."

"What time does it get dark at Nome?" My husband pushed a penciled message back to me. . . .

I passed my scribbled message forward. The lights blinked on in the front cockpit. I read by my own light the reply, "Arrive in about 1½ hours—don't lite flares until plane circles and blinks lites."

An hour and a half more! It would be night when we landed! Turned inland, we were over the mountains now and there were peaks ahead. It was darker over the land than over the water. Valleys hoard darkness as coves hoard light. Reservoirs of darkness, all through the long day they guard

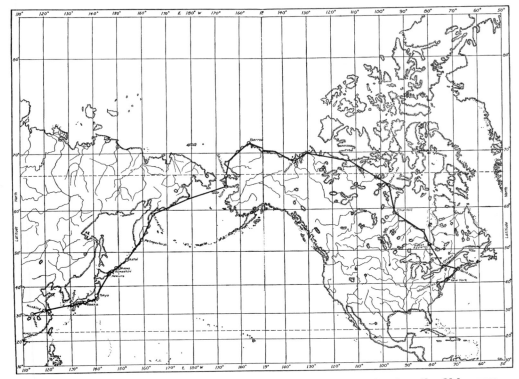

A map of the survey flight to the Far East, which ended prematurely when the Sirius was damaged in the flooded waters of the Yangtze River at Nanking. Below: Lindbergh gingerly walks the wing of the plane as it sits on the deck of the British carrier *Hermes*.

SIRIUS TROUBLE IN THE YANGTZE

In September 1931, the Lindberghs interrupted their trip to the Orient to assist victims of the flooded Yangtze River. When treacherous currents made mooring their Sirius seaplane impossible, the Lindberghs accepted an invitation to use the British carrier *Hermes* as their base of operations. Each of these recently discovered snapshots, reportedly taken by a crew member of the *Hermes,* is accompanied by the "title" penciled on its back. In sequence they show the Lindberghs' arrival and greeting on board the carrier; the preparation and hoisting of the Sirius into the river prior to one of their relief flights; and the seaplane's capsizing and subsequent retrieval. The accident, coupled with the death of Anne's father, forced the Lindberghs to cut short their expedition.

1. "When they first came on board"

2. "Colonel & Mrs. Lindbergh being driven round the flying deck in a car"

3. "Plane being prepared for flying"

4. "Plane going overboard"

"Plane being lowered"

6. "Before being hoisted"

"Plane capsized in the water"

8. "Lindbergh hooking plane to crane"

"Plane being hoisted after crash"

10. "After the crash—plane on board"

Baby Charles on his first birthday, June 22, 1931. His proud father called him "Buster."

what is left them from the night before; but now their cups were filling up, trembling at the brim, ready to spill over. The wave of night climbed up behind us; gathering strength from every crevice, it towered over us.

Suddenly my husband pulled the plane up into a stall, throttled the engine, and, in the stillness that followed, shouted back to me, "Tell him there's fog on the mountains ahead. We'll land for the night and come into Nome in the morning."

"All right, where are we?"

"Don't know exactly—northwest coast of Seward Peninsula."

Without switching on the light I started tapping rapidly, "WXN—WXN—WXN—fog—on—mountains—ahead—will—land—for—night—and—come—into—Nome—morning—position—northwest—coast—Seward—Peninsula," I repeated twice.

"Hurry up! Going to land," came a shout from the front cockpit. We were banking steeply.

No time to try again. No time to listen for reply. I did not know if they had received it, but we could not wait to circle again. We must land before that last thread of light had gone.

Down, down, down, the cold air whistling through the cowlings as we dived toward the lagoon. I must wind in the antenna before we hit the water. The muscles in my arms stiffened to soreness turning the wheel at top speed, as though I were reeling in a gigantic fish from the bottom of the sea. One more turn—*jiggle, snap*, the ball-weight clicked into place—all wound up, safe. Now—brace yourself for the landing. How *can* he see anything! Spank, spank, spank. There we go—I guess we're all right! But the ship shot on through the water—on and on. Must have landed "down wind." Now it eased up a little. There, I sighed with relief. We were taxiing toward that dark indistinct line ahead—a shore. About half a mile off my husband pulled back the throttle, idled the engine for a few seconds, then cut the switch. In the complete stillness that followed, he climbed out on to the pontoon.

"Think we'd better anchor here." He uncoiled the rope and threw out our anchor. Splash! There it stayed under about three feet of water with the rope floating on top. Heavens! Pretty shallow—thought we had more room than that. Well, we were anchored anyway. We were down—we were safe. Somewhere out on the wild coast of Seward Peninsula.

Daily, the fabulous flying Lindberghs made the front pages and rotogravure sections of newspapers around the world. Here they were eating reindeer meat with Eskimos, being received by the prime minister of Japan, meeting with Chinese president Chiang Kai-shek, flying relief missions on the flooded Yangtze River.

The expedition ended suddenly and on a black note. The seaplane flipped while being lowered from the British aircraft carrier *Hermes* into the swiftly flowing Yangtze, causing Charles and Anne to jump for their lives into the muddy current. While awaiting repairs, word reached them that Dwight Morrow had died unexpectedly of a stroke. Charles cancelled the balance of the trip and returned with Anne via ship and rail connections to the states.

The country joined the family in mourning the passing of the fifty-eight-year-old patriarch, who had been elected to the Senate a year earlier and was rumored to be a possible Republican candidate for the presidency. The *New York Times* ran a front-page obituary and the vice president was one of 4,000 people at his funeral. Her father's death left a large void in Anne's life, one that little Charlie helped fill.

That winter, Charles and Anne completed moving into the home that they'd had built on a heavily wooded 425-acre site near Hopewell, New Jersey. Compared to the Morrow and Guggenheim estates, the whitewashed stone house was too small and austere to qualify as a mansion. (It cost $80,000, one-fifth of what the Morrows had spent to build Next Day Hill.) Nonetheless, the double-winged structure was impressive, containing multiple bedrooms and studies, a nursery, and servants quarters. More important to Charles was the house's isolation. The surrounding area was mostly uninhabited and largely inaccessible.

Charles was not quite thirty, yet his fame had grown to the point that it knew no bounds and recognized no borders. Following the lead of American music publishers, songwriters in Italy, Panama, Japan, Belgium, France, Germany, Great Britain, Turkey, Sweden, Cuba, and the Netherlands released tunes saluting the various stages of his already crowded life: the flight to Paris, his Latin American tour, his marriage to Anne, the birth of their "Eaglet," their trip to the Orient. "Even three and a half years after his flight," Frederick Lewis Allen noted at the time, "the roads about his New Jersey farm were blocked on weekends with the cars of admirers who wanted to catch a glimpse of him, and it was said that he could not even send his shirts to a laundry because they did not come back—they were too valuable as souvenirs. His picture hung in hundreds of schoolrooms and in thousands of houses. No living American—no dead American, one might almost say, save perhaps Abraham Lincoln—commanded such unswerving fealty. You might criticize Coolidge or Hoover or Ford or Edison or Bobby Jones or any other headline hero; but if you decried anything that Lindbergh did, you knew that you had wounded your auditors. For Lindbergh was a god."

A Greek god, Allen might have added, to whom a tragedy of classical proportions was about to happen.

One Sunday in February 1932, America's cowboy philosopher, Will Rogers, dropped in on the Lindberghs. "The Lindbergh baby is the cutest thing you ever saw," Rogers reported in his syndicated column, "walking, talking, and disgraced the Lindbergh name by crying to come away with Mrs. Rogers and I in the car."

A few columns later, the country's most popular humorist somberly revisited that afternoon for his readers. He recalled "the affection of the mother and father and the whole Morrow family for the cute little fellow."

> Two weeks ago Sunday Mrs. Rogers and I spent the day with them. The whole family interest centered around him. He had his father's blonde curly hair, even more so than his dad's. It's almost golden and all in little curls. His face is more of his mother's. He has her eyes exactly.
>
> His mother sat on the floor in the sun parlor among all of us and played blocks with him for an hour. His dad was pitching a soft sofa pillow at him as he was toddling around. The weight of it would knock him over. I asked Lindy if he was rehearsing him for forced landings.
>
> After about the fourth time of being knocked over he did the cutest thing. He dropped of his own accord when he saw it coming. He was just stumbling and jabbering around like any kid 20 months old.
>
> He crawled up in the back of the Morrow automobile that was going to take us home, and he howled like an Indian when they dragged him out.

There was a stark difference in the circumstances surrounding the writing of the first column and its follow-up. At the time the latter was written, the subject of Rogers's affectionate reminiscence—the bubbly, inquisitive child that Anne had lovingly dubbed "the fat lamb" and Charles called "Buster"—had been missing from his crib for several days.

"I wish," concluded Rogers, "we had taken him home with us and kept him."

THELMA MILLER

"It just goes on and on"

While generations of ordinary Americans have been fascinated by the story of Charles Lindbergh's life, few have preserved his triumphs and tragedies with the fidelity of Thelma Miller. The Three Bridges, New Jersey, native has eighteen scrapbooks filled with yellowed clippings of the famous aviator, a paper trail that stretches back more than seventy years.

I started keeping a scrapbook on Lindbergh when he crossed the Atlantic in 1927. I was ten years old at the time. My mother and grandmother started clipping out articles. My mother used to keep scrapbooks, and I guess that's where I got my enjoyment out of doing it, too. Any newspaper or magazine article that we could get our hands on. We didn't get too many papers, because we didn't have too much money to buy anything with, you know. Some of the stories were from local papers, some were from the bigger newspapers. Why'd we do it? Well, he was a brave young man, a nice looking fellow. Crossing the ocean was something so important. The scrapbooks probably weren't that unique at the time. There were more than a few girls who had a schoolgirl crush on him.

I was born and raised in Three Bridges, about three miles from Flemington. We had 110 acres, grew all sorts of grains, potatoes. My father, David Kline, was a policeman in Flemington. He was on the street. This was before the days when policemen drove around in cars. He was well liked. He used to go up and down the streets, walking his beat, talking to people, taking care of problems.

Lindbergh is escorted to court by Thelma Miller's father, Deputy David Kline (left) and the chief of the New Jersey State Police, Colonel H. Norman Schwarzkopf.

Thelma Miller today: a lifetime of Lindy.

After the Lindberghs got married, they bought the estate in Hopewell, New Jersey, right over the Sourland Mountains and about twenty-five miles from where we were. I can't remember my exact reaction about that, but I'm sure we thought it was great. Here was this great hero living practically in our backyard.

The kidnapping—well, we all thought it was terrible, of course. And everybody was kind of scared. I mean, somebody's going around, kidnapping a child. We all hoped that they would catch whoever did it. I mean, who would do such a thing? Some local criminal, we figured. I remember parents with young children wouldn't venture out because the police would stop

them, looking for the Lindbergh baby.

After the police caught Hauptmann, the trial was held in Flemington. This was in the early part of 1935, winter. It was cold and snowy. The town changed overnight. Loads of people. Flemington became world famous. Our family was one of the few who didn't take in boarders. Our farm was too far away, three miles away. My father was one of Hauptmann's guards in his jail cell. He was up there all the time. He'd come home sometimes to change his clothes. Back and forth. He'd come home, tell us a few things about what was going on, then go back to the jail.

Pop said that when Hauptmann

was in his cell, he would climb up and down the bars for exercise. All news of the trial was cut out of the newspapers before they were given to Hauptmann to read. Pop said he was a model prisoner, never gave them a hard time. The only time he broke down and cried was when his wife, Anna, brought their son in to see him. His eating utensils were always made of cardboard instead of metal, to prevent his suicide, I guess.

I was a student at Flemington High School at the time. Pop gave me two tickets to attend the trial. I sat in the balcony and the two witnesses I saw were Dr. Condon and the wood expert, Arthur Koehler. My younger brother, Lambert, had a pass and someone wanted to buy it, so he sold it for twenty-five dollars. That was a whole lot of money in 1935.

I saw Hauptmann and Lindbergh sitting there. They weren't too far apart from each other. Lindbergh always stared straight ahead. He very seldom carried on a conversation. Lindbergh always left his hat and jacket in the car and went to court through the jail to avoid the people. He carried a gun in his hip pocket. You could see the impression in his pants where he had his pistol.

Hauptmann would sometimes talk to his wife, but there was always a state trooper between them. They weren't supposed to touch each other or be too close. I've got pictures of Hauptmann in my scrapbooks that show him as being kind of tough and unruly, but in court he was always neat and well-groomed. His hair was always combed and he had nice looking clothes. He wasn't a bad looking man.

I remember there was a man standing on the courthouse steps, selling these special souvenir pennies. He'd stamp a tin cover on top of a 1935 penny. The wording said, "Hauptmann Trial, Flemington, New Jersey." He was selling them for ten cents apiece. This being the depression, we were poor. We didn't have extra money so we never thought about buying one. A few years ago, I bought a couple for twenty dollars. I don't know what they're worth now.

When the jury reached a decision, they rang the courthouse bell eight times, meaning the verdict was in. Was he guilty? Oh, sure. Pop thought they had the right man. I think everybody around here that attended the trial, heard the evidence, thought Hauptmann was guilty. After that the town was empty. We were glad. Too much commotion.

I got married in 1937. I didn't pay too much attention to Lindbergh during the war. But I kept the clippings, about his speeches and the whole controversy. I added to them all through the years, when they made the movie and his conservation work later on. When he died in Hawaii, I was sad. I cried. I mean, this has been my life for quite a while. So I cried.

I have eighteen giant scrapbooks. I don't know about the fascination over the trial, or over his life. I can't explain it. This whole Lindbergh thing, it just goes on and on.

Keepsakes signifying a hero's triumph and tragedy: a watch commemorating the flight to Paris and a stamped penny from the Hauptmann trial.

WANTED

INFORMATION AS TO THE WHEREABOUTS OF

CHAS. A. LINDBERGH, Jr.

OF HOPEWELL, N. J.

SON OF COL. CHAS. A. LINDBERGH

World-Famous Aviator

This child was kidnaped from his home in Hopewell, N. J., between 8 and 10 p. m. on Tuesday, March 1, 1932.

DESCRIPTION:

Age, 20 months
Weight, 27 to 30 lbs.
Height, 29 inches
Hair, blond, curly
Eyes, dark blue
Complexion, light
Deep dimple in center of chin
Dressed in one-piece coverall night suit

ADDRESS ALL COMMUNICATIONS TO
COL. H. N. SCHWARZKOPF, TRENTON, N. J., or
COL. CHAS. A. LINDBERGH, HOPEWELL, N. J.

ALL COMMUNICATIONS WILL BE TREATED IN CONFIDENCE

March 11, 1932

COL. H. NORMAN SCHWARZKOPF
Supt. New Jersey State Police, Trenton, N. J.

CHAPTER SIX

Stolen in the Night

I n February 1932, Charles and Anne were settling into their new home and a routine. They spent weekdays at the Morrow estate in Englewood, which was more convenient to Charles's daily forays into New York and allowed Anne time with her family, and weekends at their recently completed house on the outskirts of Hopewell. They rarely deviated from this schedule, something that would have been evident to anybody tracing their movements. However, on the last Monday of the month, with the family battling a cold, Charles decided to delay their departure for Englewood. He drove in alone to New York while Anne and the baby stayed home. Anne called her mother to let her know of the change in plans.

The following morning, Tuesday, March 1, 1932, mother and son were feeling better but were still sniffling. The damp weather convinced Charles that it would be best for them to stay put. "Let's give Buster another day indoors," he said.

Anne updated her mother by telephone. She also asked if one of the Morrow chauffeurs could drive nursemaid Betty Gow from Next Day Hill, where she had been expecting the Lindberghs since Monday, to Hopewell. Gow arrived in the early afternoon and was soon playing with Charlie in the second-floor nursery in the southeast corner of the house. By the time she and Anne fed the baby and dressed him for bed, Anne had decided that everybody was healthy enough to make the trip to Englewood the next morning. At about 7:30 Charlie was placed in the crib, his thumb guards on and his blanket secured to the mattress with safety pins. All the windows in the room were closed and shuttered except one, which was warped. The lights were turned off. Outside, the winter wind howled.

While Anne went downstairs to the living room to wait for Charles to come back from a long day at the Rockefeller Institute, Gow spent the next half-hour in the bathroom adjacent to the nursery, cleaning up. At 8 o'clock she checked in on Charlie, cracking open a French window before leaving the room and shutting the door behind her. She told Anne he was sound asleep. Gow then went to the west wing—the opposite side of the house—to have her supper in the kitchen with Oliver and Elsie Whatley, the Lindberghs' only other house servants.

About 8:10 P.M., Anne heard what she thought was the crunching of tires on the gravel driveway, an indication that Charles had returned from New York. However, it wasn't until fifteen minutes later that Charles honked the car horn to signal his arrival. He went upstairs and washed his hands in the bathroom next to the nursery, then returned downstairs for a late supper without looking in on the baby. Afterwards, he

The Lindberghs' estate near Hopewell, New Jersey. The second-story nursery is at far right, under the gabled roof. Later, police used a ladder to reconstruct the crime.

and Anne went into the living room. In the midst of their conversation, sometime after 9 o'clock, Charles heard an odd cracking noise. It was similar, he later said, to the sound of a dropped crate. Passing it off as coming from the kitchen, he resumed their talk. Around 9:15 they went upstairs. Charles took a bath, then went downstairs to his study directly under the nursery. Anne stayed in their bedroom, reading, then drew a bath.

As was her custom, Gow went to check on the baby at 10 o'clock before retiring for the night. There was an uncomfortable chill in the room. She closed the window and turned on the electric heater. As she approached the crib in the semidarkness she gradually became aware of a frightening silence. She could not hear Charlie breathing.

Gow ran her hands over the bedcovers, thinking perhaps the baby had slipped beneath them. The blanket was still pinned in place, but the crib was empty.

She hurried down the corridor into the master bedroom. Anne had just stepped out of the bathroom. "Do you have the baby, Mrs. Lindbergh?" she asked anxiously.

"No," she said. "Maybe the Colonel has him."

Racing downstairs to the study, Gow confronted Charles at his desk. She was aware of his penchant for practical jokes. "Do you have the baby, Colonel? Don't fool me."

"No," he said, startled. "Isn't he in his crib?"

"No," said Gow.

Charles bolted upstairs. He looked into the empty crib, then searched the other rooms. He grabbed a rifle out of his bedroom closet.

"Anne," he said, "they have stolen our baby."

Charles immediately contacted several law enforcement agencies, including the state police post in Trenton. News of the kidnapping was put on the teletype, launching what was to become the largest manhunt in American history.

"It was still pitch black when we got there," recalled Francis Larson, one of the many state troopers who were soon pouring over the crime scene. "There was so much confusion all over. Everybody was searching. Everybody was looking. Everybody was talking."

Three sections of a ladder were found about seventy-five feet from the house. Judging by imprints in the mud, the kidnapper had used the ladder to climb through the second-floor nursery window. The middle section had a splintered side rail; the noise Charles had heard but not investigated evidently had been the sound of cracking wood. The ladder, along with the ransom note that Charles had discovered on top of the nursery's radiator, were dusted for fingerprints. There were none. The kidnapper had worn gloves.

The ransom note demanded $50,000:

dear Sir!
    Have 50.000 $ redy 25 000 $ in
20 $ bills 15000 $ in 10 $ bills and
10000 $ in 5 $ bills. After 2-4 days
we will inform you were to deliver
the Mony.
    We warn you for making
anyding public or for notify the Police
    the child is in gut care.
    Indication for all letters are
singnature
              and 3 holes.

Detectives theorized that the author of the note probably was of German or Scandinavian origin. More baffling was the "signature" in the bottom right corner: a red solid circle joining two interlocking blue circles, punctuated by a line of three squarish holes.

The Lindberghs' estate was turned into headquarters for the investigation. Police installed a twenty-line switchboard to handle the flood of incoming and outgoing calls, while a small army of men representing various local, state, and federal agencies investigated leads, interviewed witnesses, guarded the property from the growing throngs of reporters and gawkers, and went through the hundreds of letters arriving daily. "It is impossible to describe the confusion," Anne wrote Charles's mother, "—a police station downstairs by day—detectives, police, secret service men swarming in

The nursery a few days after the baby's abduction and the ransom note left behind on the window ledge.

and out—mattresses all over the dining room and other rooms at night. At any time I may be routed out of my bed so that a group of detectives may have a conference in the room. It is so terrifically unreal that I do not feel anything."

After two days had passed with no further word from the kidnappers, Charles released an open letter to the press:

> Mrs. Lindbergh and I desire to make a personal contact with the kidnapers (*sic*) of our child.
>
> Our only interest is in his immediate and safe return and we feel certain that the kidnapers will realize that this interest is strong enough to justify them in having complete confidence and trust in any promises that we may make in connection with his return.
>
> We urge those who have the child to select any representatives of ours who will be suitable to them at any time and at any place that they may designate.
>
> If this is accepted, we promise that we will keep whatever arrangements that may be made by their representative and ours strictly confidential and we further pledge ourselves that we will not try to injure in any way those connected with the return of the child.

Anne, determined to stay as optimistic as her husband, released the baby's daily diet, including "½ cup of prune juice after the afternoon nap" and "14 drops of medicine called Viosterola during the day." Meanwhile, the *New York Times* wrote, "The world waits hopefully."

The lawman in charge was H. Norman Schwarzkopf, the thirty-seven-year-old founder and superintendent of the New Jersey State Police (and father of the future Gulf War hero-general). Although Charles had no official authority in the case (his offer of immunity to the kidnappers was immediately criticized by the state attorney general), his energy, level-headed intensity, and larger-than-life persona allowed him to essentially take over the investigation. Most of the people working on the case clearly were in awe of Lindbergh. Schwarzkopf, an authoritative but congenial type who quickly grew close to the Lindberghs, often deferred to his suggestions and demands.

On March 5, the kidnappers contacted Lindbergh via a second ransom note. "We have warned you note to make anyding Public also notify the Police," it read. "Now you have to take the consequences." Stating that the baby was being fed according to Anne's diet and that they wished "to send him back in gut health," they upped their demand to $70,000. The note went on to say that the Lindberghs would be notified as to how the money should be delivered, but not until "the Polise is out of this cace and the Papers are quite."

This was an impossibility. As reporters, photographers, newsreel cameramen, radio commentators, sightseers, vendors, publicity hounds, and assorted quacks overran the small town of Hopewell, Charles found himself in the eye of the media storm for the second time in five years. Once again, his life was a national drama, played out in tabloid fashion as the public clamored to find out every last scrap of information about the crime, the investigation, and anybody even peripherally involved. The Hearst organization fueled the frenzy by cranking out 30,000 words a day; the slight-

Al Capone, flanked by his attorneys inside a federal courtroom in Chicago, offered his help in finding the kidnappers.

ly more subdued Associated Press put another 10,000 words over the wire. Speculation ran rampant, reported the *New York Times*, one of the few newspapers Lindbergh felt acted responsibly. "No story was too fantastic for investigation. No suspected place was too remote for search." There was profit in misery. Publishers across the country saw their circulations soar an average of 20 percent in the three weeks following the kidnapping.

Al Capone contributed to the surging sales by offering to use all of his underworld connections to locate the child. America's most celebrated gangster, who had a photo of his thirteen-year-old son inside his cell, saw an opportunity to play the hero and to curry favor with the federal government, which had just sentenced him to eleven years for income tax evasion. "I will give any bond they require if they are interested in the child," he told Hearst editor Arthur Brisbane. "I will spend every hour of the night and day with Thomas Callaghan, head of the United States Secret Service. The Government knows that it can trust him, I think, and I will send my young brother to stay here in the jail until I come back. You don't suppose anybody would suggest that I would double-cross my own brother and leave him here, if I could get away from Callaghan?"

Lindbergh conferred with the agents of the Internal Revenue Service responsible for putting the crime lord behind bars. Their advice was to ignore Capone, whose influence had waned. More useful than Scarface, they thought, would be Lucky Luciano. As repulsive as the idea of dealing with underworld figures seemed to many, Charles and Anne rationalized that at least they were *professionals*, which in kidnapping, as in any other line of work, counted for something. Kidnapping had long been a favorite criminal activity, with ransom victims rarely being harmed. In 1931 alone, nearly three hundred people around the country had been snatched and safely returned, many of them children of the affluent and powerful. Hundreds more cases went unreported. With all this in mind, Charles publicly authorized two members of the New York underworld, Salvy Spitale and Irving Bitz, to act as intermediaries, should the abductors wish to avoid dealing directly with him. Meanwhile, several hundred miles away, interrogations of Detroit's notorious Purple Gang turned up nothing that suggested a hometown angle to the crime.

In the Bronx, Dr. John F. Condon was keeping abreast of these latest developments and growing incensed. Born at the outbreak of the Civil War, the retired teacher with the distinctive white walrus mustache had aged into an eccentric moralist and super-patriot who signed his regular correspondence to the *Bronx Home News* as "J. U. Stice" and "P. A. Triot." To Condon, the Lone Eagle was an idol for the ages

Because of the Lindberghs' ties to Detroit, suspicion immediately fell upon members of the city's Purple Gang, which had staked out a national reputation as bootleggers, kidnappers, and killers-for-hire. Trying to stay optimistic, Anne wrote her mother-in-law on April 29, 1932: "I should love to have the baby turn up in Detroit, in your quiet home. Of course anywhere would be wonderful." Three weeks later, the child was found dead.

VIOLET SHARPE IN MYSTERY TRYST

Violet Placed Here

On Stand:

DIED IN VAIN

Hauptmann Case Witnesses

DEFENDS THE DEAD

To Be Cleared

VIOLET SHARPE.

"JUST COFFEE"

The pages of America's press were filled with endless gossip and speculation, adding to the Lindberghs' ordeal. Anne admitted to "nausea at the sight of newspapers."

and the kidnapping a national disgrace. If extortion of such a hero was inevitable, at least let the intermediary be a man of unquestioned honor, integrity, and morality—in short, someone like himself. He wrote a letter to the paper, declaring his wish to the kidnappers to act as a go-between in the case. He even offered to kick in $1,000 of his own savings towards the ransom. "I stand ready at my own expense to go anywhere, alone, to give the kidnapper the extra money and promise never to utter his name to any person," he wrote.

Incredibly, the kidnappers responded. On March 8, a day after his letter was published, Condon received a note with the distinctive hole-punched symbol on the bottom. It ordered that an ad be placed in the *New York American* as a sign that the ransom money was ready to be turned over. In order to disguise Condon's identity, all communications were to be signed "Jafsie," an acronym made from his initials.

By now, authorities had more or less resigned themselves to Lindbergh's running the show. Despite an outward show of optimism, Schwarzkopf privately believed the baby was dead, as did the top detective on the case. Experience had taught them that kidnappers invariably threatened violence to the victim in their ransom notes; there was none of that from whoever had snatched little Charlie from his crib. Schwarzkopf objected but didn't interfere as Condon—acting with Lindbergh's blessings and upon further instructions given to him by the kidnappers—kept a late-night rendezvous on March 12 at Woodlawn Cemetery in the Bronx. There he and a man hidden in the shadows negotiated for more than an hour. The stranger spoke with a handkerchief to his mouth, muffling what sounded like a thick German accent. The man finally agreed to produce the baby's sleep suit as proof that he actually had the child before the Lindberghs paid the ransom. Schwarzkopf was angry with Charles for prohibiting any officers from tailing Condon. As a result, the mystery man Condon dubbed "Cemetery John" had gotten away, disappearing like an apparition among the tombstones.

Throughout this time, the Lindberghs were deluged with up to 700 letters a day, each of which was carefully examined by the police. By early April they had received 38,000 pieces of mail, which were sorted by contents: 12,000 dreams, 11,500 sympathy, 9,500 suggestions, and 5,000 cranks. For a while they had to contend with sight-

A hearse bearing the baby's body makes its way through the throngs gathered outside Walter Swayze's funeral parlor in Trenton.

seeing planes operating from a nearby airfield; for $2.50 a ticket, rubberneckers could gawk at the beelike activity around the Lindbergh estate and maybe even catch a glimpse of the famous parents.

Hundreds of nuts came out of their shells. A woman named Greta Gray was representative. She traveled all the way from Minnesota, claiming to be an acquaintance of the aviator's mother and the holder of valuable information concerning the kidnapping. Despite her dubious claims, she was put through on the telephone to Charles.

"This is Colonel Lindbergh's secretary," he said. "You say you knew Mrs. Lindbergh?"

"Yes," Gray replied, "in Minneapolis."

"Oh, then that was when she was living in Minneapolis?"

"Yes, that was it."

"Did you know her very well?"

"Oh, not very well, but I used to see her quite often when she lived in Minneapolis."

"But, you know," said Charles, "she never lived in Minneapolis."

Caught in her lie, the woman could only blurt, "Oh, I wish you hadn't asked me that question."

The criminal, the delusional—Charles was willing to entertain all types in order to get his boy back. Anne, several months pregnant, stayed out of the way. She spent much of her time crying in her room. Her family feared grief would cause a miscarriage.

Several days after Condon's nocturnal meeting with Cemetery John, the baby's gray sleep suit—freshly laundered—arrived in the mail, along with a note demanding immediate payment of the ransom. On the evening of April 2, following an exchange of secret messages in the newspapers, Condon approached St. Raymond's Cemetery in the East Bronx. From out of the darkness came the shout "Hey, Doktor!"—a cry which Lindbergh later claimed he heard distinctly, though he was sitting in a parked car a couple hundred feet away.

Condon recognized the man standing behind a hedge as Cemetery John. "Have you gotted the money?" he asked. Condon did: $70,000 in easily traceable gold certificates, their serial numbers recorded by the police, that had been packed into two boxes. Condon actually was able to talk the man out of $20,000. In exchange for the box containing $50,000, he received a sealed envelope with information on where to find the baby.

The handwritten note said:

the boy is on Boad Nelly. it is a small Boad
28 feet long. two persons are on the Boad. the
are innosent. you will find the Boad between
Horseneck Beach and gay Head near Elizabeth
Island.

Charles struggled to control his excitement. He had fufilled his end of the bargain, keeping the police and the press out of the loop as he promised the kidnappers he would, and now they would honor their promise to return his son safely. The next day he flew low over the waters between Martha's Vineyard and the Massachusetts coast in a borrowed Navy seaplane, looking for a boat named *Nelly*. He brought along the boy's favorite blanket in anticipation of their reunion. Coast Guard vessels participated in the search. By nightfall, it was clear that no such boat existed. Charles dejectedly stated the obvious. "We've been double-crossed." He returned to Hopewell empty-handed, save for the blanket.

In early April, marked ransom bills began popping up around the East Side of New York. The leads quickly turned cold. Throughout the rest of the month and into May, no further word was heard from whoever had taken—and was now spending—the $50,000 from Jafsie.

• • •

At 3:15 on the afternoon of May 12, 1932, the search for the Lindbergh baby came to an end. Forty-six-year-old William Allen, traveling with a friend along the Hopewell-Mt. Rose Highway a couple of miles southeast of Hopewell, had stopped to relieve himself in the woods. "I went under a branch and looked down," he said. "I saw a skull sticking up out of the dirt, which seemed to have been kicked up around it. I thought I saw a baby, with its foot sticking out of the ground." Within minutes the police had been informed and were swarming around the shallow grave. It was roughly four miles from the Lindberghs' house.

The mangled, blackened corpse was obviously that of an infant. Judging by its condition, it had been there for a long time. The left hand, the lower left leg, and much of the right arm had been gnawed off by wild animals, and most of the internal organs were missing. Despite the advanced state of decay, Charlie was still recognizable by his blonde curls, blue eyes, dimpled chin, and clothing. A bloodstained burlap bag was found nearby. After nearly seventy years, the experience still affects Francis Larson, then a twenty-five-year-old trooper assigned to the Lindberghs' house. "I've seen a lot of bad things in my time," he reflected. "But if you have children, you can't realize what it is like until you lose one."

In the wake of their son's murder, the Lindberghs found solitude in the sky.

The body was taken by ambulance to the Swayze & Margerum funeral home in Trenton for the autopsy. The coroner determined that the cause of death was "a fractured skull due to extreme violence." Because there were no other visible wounds, detectives theorized that the kidnapper had placed the baby in the burlap bag and, while descending the ladder, slipped when the side rail cracked. The baby's head banged against the thick concrete wall, a blow that undoubtedly killed him instantly.

Betty Gow and the family's pediatrician each made a positive identification. The following day Charles did as well, but not before one final indignity was inflicted on the boy. Overnight, a photographer broke into the morgue and took a picture of the remains. Soon copies of the morbid photograph were being hawked on the streets of Trenton for five dollars apiece.

Charles was enraged. What kind of men *were* these? They couldn't possibly be human. They were more like jackals, feeding off other people's misery and respecting no claims to privacy or simple decency. Along with the outrage was a feeling of degradation. Throughout the seventy-two-day ordeal of trying to get his son safely back, Charles had been betrayed by others who had wormed their way into his confidence.

The cruelest hoax was that of John Hughes Curtis, owner of a failing boat company in Norfolk, Virginia. Curtis maintained that, thanks to some bootlegging connections, he could lead Lindbergh to the boat that the baby was being held on. At a time when hopes for Charlie's safe return were dwindling, desperation forced Charles to ignore Schwarzkopf's and his own misgivings and trust this barely credible source. Nearly every day for three weeks Lindbergh and Curtis sailed around aimlessly, with Curtis offering an unending stream of excuses for why they could not yet meet up with the abductors. As Betty Gow later said, Charles's behavior caused Anne for the first time to realize that she had married a mortal, not an infallible god.

Charles was out at sea with Curtis that drizzly Thursday when word came that Charlie's corpse had been found. Curtis, his lie exposed a few days later, begged for forgiveness. Facing prosecution for obstruction of justice (he ultimately would serve a year in prison), he sobbed that he had needed money, that he had wanted to become famous. Lindbergh was revolted. "Filth!" he said.

The public response to the murder was that of overwhelming sympathy. In what was described as the greatest demonstration of collective grief since the North mourned Lincoln's assassination, people sent hundreds of bouquets and more than 100,000 written and telegraphed condolences to the Lindberghs. Many enclosed holy cards and maudlin poetry. Music publishers capitalized on the nation's sorrow, releasing songs like "The Eaglet is Dead," "Bring My Darling Baby Back" and "The Mystery Murder of Baby Lindbergh" (written by a woman named Butcher, no less).

Given the morbid voyeurism of the public, a gravesite was out of the question. The body was cremated. One day that summer, with the hysteria now largely spent, Charles climbed into an airplane and flew alone out over the Atlantic. Only Anne knew the nature of the flight. In an elemental communion of fire, sky, wind, and water, he strewed the ashes of their son. The ceremony was sad but satisfying. Nobody would ever be able to violate little Buster again.

• • •

With the baby's body found, law enforcement agencies alternately cooperated and competed with each other to be the one that found his murderer. While Charles remained as strong and immutable as a rock, Anne was reduced to an anthill of ash. She spent hours sitting in the empty nursery, running her hands over her dead baby's clothes and toys. She seemed unable to break out of a deep, melancholic funk.

"They talk and talk, conferences, discussions," she confided to her diary. "But I am so tired of the talking. What difference does it make now?" The next day, following yet another police reconstruction of the crime, she complained: "We are building backwards, not forwards. I feel as if it were a poison working in my system, this idea of the crime. How deep will it eat into our lives?"

On August 16, 1932, Anne gave birth to a boy, an event that lifted her from her spiraling depression. He was given a Scandinavian name, Jon. The Lindberghs, convinced that publicity had contributed to the death of their first son, prevailed upon the press to give the family some breathing room. The press backed off, but the Lindberghs could do nothing about the cranks that wandered onto their property or sent threatening letters. Finally, Charles and Anne decided to give up Hopewell for good. They donated the house and the grounds to the state for use as a sanctuary for children and moved into the Morrow estate.

Over the next two years, as the search for the murderer dragged on and Congress passed legislation that made kidnapping a federal offense punishable by death (it inevitably became known as the Lindbergh Law), Charles and Anne immersed them-

Anne Morrow Lindbergh in the cockpit of the Sirius in 1933. A young Eskimo painted the name "Tingmissartoq" on the fuselage. It means "the one who flies like a big bird."

selves in a variety of research, aviation, and creative projects. Along with their nurturing of a new child inside the safe and familiar harbor of Next Day Hill, the activities helped keep the dark memories at bay. Anne worked on her first book, *North to the Orient*, an account of the 1931 flight to Japan and China; it was destined to become the year's top-selling nonfiction title when published in 1935. Its unexpected success would encourage the fledgling, unsure writer to begin a second book-length manuscript. This one was based on the journals she kept during the pioneering survey of transatlantic air routes she and Charles made for Pan American in 1933.

That grueling five-month flight was made in the Lockheed Sirius seaplane they had flown to Asia. The voyage covered 30,000 miles in all: from New Jersey to Greenland, Iceland, Scandinavia, Russia, and Great Britain, then south to Spain and West Africa, a hop across the Atlantic to Brazil, and then back to the states via the Caribbean and Miami. Once again, Anne served as navigator and radio operator as Charles expertly piloted through every kind of extreme weather, including blizzards, sandstorms, and tropical storms. For Lady Lindbergh, much of the trip was sheer terror. Apart from the physical fear that she felt for the first time in the air, there was the haunting, howling wind that reminded her of the night little Charlie had been stolen. The most agonizing aspect of the trip was the time she spent separated from Jon. Charles, on the other hand, enjoyed himself immensely, as he always did when the challenge was great. The mapping and scientific data collected on the flight allowed

Greenland, where the Lindberghs spent twenty-four days in the summer of 1933.

Pan Am to start seriously planning regular passenger service. It also prompted the National Geographic Society to confer the Hubbard Gold Medal on Anne, the first woman explorer so honored.

When Charles wasn't busy plotting new air routes or testing equipment, he con-

Anne and Charles in the Shetland Islands during their 1933 survey flight.

tinued his equally pathbreaking work on a perfusion pump with Dr. Alexis Carrel at the Rockefeller Institute. An element of personal desperation drove Charles's experimentation into the possibilities of repairing organs outside of the body. Anne's beloved sister, Elisabeth, had suffered a series of minor heart attacks. Doctors offered little hope that the frail twenty-eight-year-old could live too many more years before her heart failed her completely. "If the circulation of blood could be maintained artificially for a few minutes," Charles mused, "why couldn't the heart be stopped and its lesions removed by the surgeon's scalpel?" Elisabeth's grim prognosis,

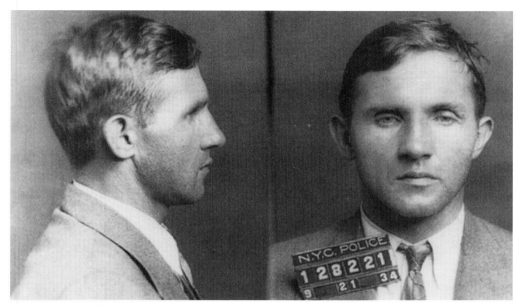

The New York City police mug shot of Bruno Richard Hauptmann.

when heaped upon the recent deaths of her father and firstborn, had a sedative effect on Anne's emotions. Try as she might, she could not shake the feeling of dread and foreboding and helplessness over "the transitory quality in life" that filled so many of her private moments.

Although Anne would have been happy living at Next Day Hill indefinitely, she knew the constant social swirl made her husband uncomfortable. They needed a place of their own. She and Charles experimented briefly with apartment living in New York, then contemplated a move to California, where Elisabeth was convalescing with her new husband, a Welshman named Aubrey Morgan. They were visiting the new-lyweds on the coast in September 1934, just months before Elisabeth slipped into her final illness, when Colonel Schwarzkopf telephoned. He told Charles that police had arrested a Bronx carpenter as a prime suspect in their son's murder and that he should return to New Jersey immediately.

"Oh, God," said Anne, "it's starting again."

"Yes," said Charles. "But they've got him at last."

•   •   •

According to H. L. Mencken, the acerbic editor of the *American Mercury*, the trial of Bruno Richard Hauptmann for the kidnap-murder of the Lindberghs's baby was the greatest story since the Resurrection of Christ. The Lindberghs, of course, were already world-famous. The man in the dock was made a celebrity by the notoriety of his crime.

As even Charles admitted, the accused was a fine-looking specimen. He was thir-ty-five years old, with a muscular build and pleasing facial features. His cold, flat eyes, however, suggested dark impulses.

Hauptmann, like so many of his generation, had been scarred by the war. Born in the Saxon village of Kamenz on November 26, 1899, he was trained as a carpenter

**New Jersey Attorney General
David T. Wilentz (left) and Dr. John
F. Condon arrive in court.**

before being conscripted into the Kaiser's army in
1917. Only eighteen, he suffered a gassing and a
head wound in combat. He was lucky to have survived; two of his brothers were killed in action.
According to Hauptmann, the war's great lesson
was that nothing in life was sacred.

Caring for his widowed mother, Hauptmann
scrambled to survive in the tumult of postwar
Germany. He committed a series of burglaries and
armed robberies, for which he served four years in
prison. On one occasion he robbed two women
pushing baby carriages; on another he climbed
through an upper-story window to steal some jew-
elry. He escaped in 1923 and came to the United
States on his third attempt as a stowaway, arriving
in Hoboken, New Jersey, with no passport and no
knowledge of the English language. He had exactly two cents to his name. Hauptmann abandoned
his plan of joining his sister in California when he
met Anna Schoeffler, a red-haired German immigrant who he said reminded him of his mother.
They married, had a child, and slowly improved
their station, thanks principally to Hauptmann's
steady work as a carpenter.

Although most of the rest of the country was
hurting because of the Great Depression, the
Hauptmanns were able to afford expensive clothes, vacations, a four-hundred-dollar
radio, and other luxuries. By the time the New Jersey State Police—working in con-
cert with the FBI and the New York City police—traced a marked ten-dollar gold cer-

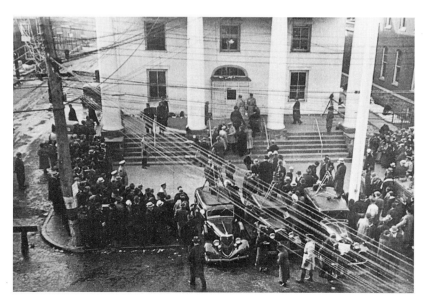

For several
weeks in early
1935, "the trial
of the century"
was played out
inside the
Hunterdon
County
Courthouse in
Flemington,
New Jersey.

The media descends on Flemington.

tificate to their comfortably furnished five-room flat in the Bronx, Hauptmann had convinced his wife and neighbors that their uncommonly high standard of living was due to his success as an investor and a businessman. The detectives who arrested him on September 19, 1934, thought otherwise.

Hauptmann never admitted to any involvement in the kidnapping, even after detectives found a marked twenty in his wallet and $14,600 of ransom money stashed in the joists of his garage. There was other incriminating evidence found in his apartment: several maps of New Jersey, an empty bottle of ether, a revolver, sketches of a ladder and two windows, and paper matching that of the ransom notes. Hauptmann's obduracy frustrated detectives. Not even an around-the-clock grilling and a severe beating—probably with a hammer—elicited a confession. Hauptmann would maintain his innocence to the very end. So would his wife, who was shocked to find out in the press that her highly secretive husband's name was Bruno. During ten years of marriage, she had only known him as Richard Hauptmann.

The trial began January 2, 1935, at the Hunterdon County courthouse in Flemington, New Jersey. Hordes of reporters and cameramen descended on the town, turning Flemington into the center of the universe for the next two months. Forty-five direct lines carried news to places as far away as Australia and Brazil. A dozen planes a day flew film to New York. In addition to sending their top reporters and columnists to cover the trial, the major dailies hired popular novelists to provide color and famous lawyers to deliver commentary. Then there were the tourists. On the Sunday after the trial opened, sixty thousand people made a family outing to this corner of New Jersey. Here was Mencken's "boob-*oisie*" in full, frightful glory: gawking at the site of the baby's discovery, buying overpriced hot dogs and dubious souvenirs from roadside vendors, waiting in line like cattle for tours of the courthouse, and rounding out the experience with a plate of Baked Beans Wilentz or a Lindy Soda inside the packed dining room of the Union Hotel.

One of the youngest representatives of the fourth estate was future Lindbergh biographer Leonard Mosley, then a teenaged copyboy for the *New York Daily Mirror.* In Mosley's memory, the atmosphere was that of "a three-ring circus . . . an obscene spectacle":

> Pictures float back into the mind of that small, clean Andrew Wyeth town of painted houses and churches reeling before the invasion of people who didn't belong. Continuous publicity in the press had whipped interest to a perfervid pitch, and everyone wanted to be there. Three hundred reporters, sketch writers, and sob sisters had flocked into Flemington and had taken over the Union Hotel, across the street from the courthouse, and every rooming house in town was bulging at the seams. Not all of the newsmen had tickets for the proceedings and were avid for ancillary and off-beat stories; and once more the flacks were there to cater to them, as they had done after the kidnaping. They shipped their clients, starlets, strip teaseuses, politicians, cafe society debutantes, across the river and set them loose among the reporters and photographers, and any marginal comment about the crime was good for a story and a picture. The pages of the newspapers were open, and everything else happening in the world took second place.
>
> Main Street, Flemington, was jammed with cars, sight-seers, candy-barkers, mendicants, and pickpockets. One of my fellow copyboys bought a stack of small envelopes of translucent paper and typed on them, "Certified veritable lock of hair from Baby Lindbergh," and surreptitiously sold the small curls they contained at five dollars each. It was noticed that his own luxuriant crop of hair grew sparser as the trial proceeded. There were autographed photographs of Colonel Lindbergh (forged) going for two dollars apiece. Two Polish prostitutes from Philadelphia arrived in town and spread the word around that they offered something over and above the usual wares of their profession: and it seemed that one had a transfer picture of the *Spirit of St. Louis* flying over Manhattan on an intimate part of her anatomy, while the other had a transfer picture of the *Spirit* flying over the Eiffel Tower. You could ride from New York to Paris with Lindy at a special cut rate.

Judge Thomas W. Trenchard, an elderly justice who had never had one of his rulings in a capital case overturned on appeal, presided in his usual slow and deliberate style. In the first two days a jury of eight men and four women, mostly working-class people with an average age of forty-four, were seated. Then the battle began.

The prosecution team was led by David T. Wilentz, the young, stylishly attired state attorney general. Wilentz quickly became a media darling, typically photographed with a cigar jammed into one corner of his mouth while he dripped colorful quotes out of the other.

The chief defense counsel was the faintly decadent Edward J. Reilly. At fifty-two, the well-known criminal attorney from Brooklyn was on the down slope of a remarkably active career that had seen him defend more than 2,000 clients; so many of them had been murder suspects that the papers dubbed him "Death House Reilly." He was big and loud and dressed like the man on the Monopoly board, coming to court in spats, striped pants and a morning coat. He suffered from alcoholism and syphilis, as well as a serious lack of conviction in his client's innocence. According to an FBI agent, Reilly "knew Hauptmann was guilty, didn't like him, and was anxious to see him get the chair." The only reasons he ostensibly was in Hauptmann's corner were the guarantee of priceless free publicity and the $25,000 retainer being paid by the *New York Journal* in exchange for the exclusive rights to Anna Hauptmann's story.

The prosecution built its case around a mountain of circumstantial evidence. Hauptmann quit his job on April 2, 1935, the day the ransom was paid. The Internal Revenue Service estimated that he had total assets of less than $5,000 before that date. Nonetheless, he still managed to spend $15,000 between then and his arrest thirty months later. Several handwriting experts identified him as the author of the ransom notes, and the accused gave an unconvincing explanation of why Dr. Condon's phone number and address had been found penciled

These enterprising youngsters formed a human ladder outside the Flemington jail in hopes of catching a glimpse of the accused kidnapper.

inside his closet. Arthur Koehler, a wood technologist with the U. S. Forestry Service, gave a riveting account of his dogged eighteen-month odyssey tracing the wood used in the kidnap ladder. Koehler testified that he had methodically narrowed his search

from a possible 40,000 mills and lumber yards across the country to the very Bronx yard that Hauptmann frequented as a carpenter—this several months before he was even a suspect. Given the opportunity to scrutinize Hauptmann's tools and home after his arrest, Koehler was then able to prove that a missing plank in the attic floor had been used in building the ladder. Also, a standard three-quarter-inch chisel had been recovered at the crime scene; the exact sort of tool was found to be the only one missing from Hauptmann's carpenter's chest. There was more . . . much more.

Lindbergh testifies.

The jury in the box.

The most powerful of the prosecution's eighty-seven witnesses were the victim's parents. Anne testified once at the beginning of the trial and appeared a second time in court a few weeks later when her mother took the stand. Otherwise, she was nowhere to be seen, preferring to remain sequestered at Next Day Hill while the press's "sob sisters" wrote movingly of the young mother's composure. They didn't know of the nightmares and crying fits that took place out of the public eye.

Charles, on the other hand, was as ubiquitous and unemotive as the courtroom furniture. He attended every day of the trial, sitting at the prosecution table a few feet away from the defendant and studiously avoiding eye contact with him. It was a sign of the universal deference shown Lindbergh that nobody ever questioned the holstered .38-caliber handgun that was clearly visible under his suit jacket. The only time he didn't wear it was when he testified.

Charles took the stand immediately after Anne and spent several hours over two days under direct and cross examination. The five hundred people packed into the century-old courthouse sat transfixed as Wilentz dramatically asked, "Whose voice was it, Colonel, that you heard in the vicinity of St. Raymond's Cemetery that night, saying 'Hey, Doctor'?"

Staring directly at Hauptmann, Charles answered coolly and evenly, "That was Hauptmann's voice."

"The minute Lindbergh 'pointed his finger' at Hauptmann," recalled Charles's counsel, Henry Breckinridge, "the trial was over. 'Jesus Christ' himself said he was convinced this was the man who killed his son. Who was anybody to doubt him or deny him justice?"

Reilly mounted a vigorous if uneven defense that made up in bombast what it lacked in plausibility. He insisted that he would prove that Hauptmann had been picking up his wife from work on the night the baby was kidnapped, and that he was at a party with friends on the evening Dr.

Anne leaves the courtroom after testifying.

Condon delivered the ransom money. Hauptmann's financial windfall, he explained, was the result of his association with a tubercular business partner, Isador Fisch, who had returned to Germany and sadly (but conveniently) died and thus was unavailable for corroboration. Unfortunately for the accused, many of the street characters Reilly dredged up to buttress these alibis were almost laughably impeachable. "Where are they getting these witnesses from?" Hauptmann asked at one point. "They're really hurting me." A dozen subpoenaed defense witnesses never bothered to show up at all.

Hauptmann did not help his own cause during the nearly eighteen hours he spent on the stand. His memory failed him too many times; when he did remember, details of his story kept changing. At times he was defiant.

"You think you're a big shot, don't you?" Wilentz declared during one contentious exchange.

Defense attorney Edward J. Reilly examines his client on the stand.

"No," said Hauptmann. "Should I cry?"

"No, certainly you shouldn't. You think you are bigger than everybody, don't you?"

"No," Hauptmann shot back. "But I know I am innocent."

"Lying, when you swear to God that you will tell the truth. Telling lies doesn't mean anything."

Hauptmann pointed a finger at Wilentz. "Stop that!" he shouted. "Stop that!"

Although few trial observers were absolutely convinced that Hauptmann had acted alone, proof of his complicity seemed beyond dispute. Wilentz addressed this issue in an impassioned four-and-a-half summation on February 12. "I know how difficult it is to believe that one person committed this crime," he told the jurors. However, that was unimportant "because if fifty people did it, if Hauptmann was one of them, that would be all there was to it. . . . All the evidence leads to Hauptmann, only to Hauptmann."

The next morning, after receiving instructions from Judge Trenchard, the jurors solemnly filed out of the courtroom to decide Hauptmann's fate. By evening what Charles later described as "a lynching crowd" of thousands had assembled outside the courthouse, laughing, shouting, carousing and making wagers on the verdict. As the hours of deliberation stretched, chants of "Kill Hauptmann! Kill the German!" filled the frosty air.

The Lindberghs awaited the outcome at Next Day Hill. Harold Nicholson, a Brit and former diplomat turned writer, was a house guest while researching a biography

Jurors exit the courthouse after delivering their verdict. The unruliness of the people surrounding the building caused Lindbergh to comment, "That was a lynching crowd."

of Dwight Morrow. He remembered that news came over the radio about 11 o'clock that evening. After ten hours of deliberation, the jury had found the accused guilty. The sentence was death.

"You have now heard," said the announcer, "the verdict in the most famous trial in all history. Bruno Hauptmann now stands guilty of one of the foulest. . . ."

Anne, pale and upset, could bear no more. "Turn that off, Charles, turn that off," she said.

Everybody went into the kitchen for glasses of ginger beer. There, principally for the benefit of his wife and his mother-in-law, both of whom appeared shaken and unsure of the verdict, Charles methodically went through the case. He was positive that authorities had arrested, tried, convicted—and would soon execute—the right man. Although tangible proof was lacking, the circumstantial evidence pointing to Hauptmann's guilt was plain and overwhelming. "It seemed to relieve all of them," Nicholson wrote. "He did it very quietly, very simply. . . . It made one feel there was no personal desire for vengeance or justification; here was the solemn process of law inexorably and impersonally punishing a culprit." Afterwards, said Nicholson, everybody went to sleep, presumably with clear consciences.

The case has never stopped fascinating professional crime experts and amateur sleuths. To many, the chief unresolved mystery involves the question of accomplices. It seems highly unlikely that Hauptmann planned and pulled off the abduction alone. Just the fact that the kidnapper knew the baby would be in Hopewell instead of at Next Day Hill suggests an inside job, someone capable of delivering last-minute information about the Lindberghs' whereabouts (and possibly even the baby itself).

The police certainly thought along those lines. Early in the investigation they focused their attention on several members of the Lindbergh and Morrow household staffs, including a young, sexually promiscuous maid named Violet Sharpe. Sharpe's conflicting and confusing testimony during several interviews made her a prime suspect, but it turned out that she had other matters to conceal, among them an abortion, a drinking problem, and an affair with the Morrows' butler. When she committed suicide by gulping some cyanide-based cleaning solvent prior to yet another police grilling (dying on the kitchen floor at the feet of the horrified Betty Morrow), newspapers seized upon it as dramatic proof of her guilt. But investigators ultimately cleared her of any involvement, as they did all of the servants. Complicating the detectives' work was Charles's refusal to allow polygraph tests of any of the hired help. He had conducted extensive background checks before hiring them. Subjecting them to a lie detector test opened up the possibility that his judgment might have been flawed or his trust misplaced. Lindbergh, in his usual self-assured fashion, was certain that neither could be the case.

'FAREWELL RICHARD'—WIFE'S LAST MESSAGE TO BRUNO HAUPTMANN

PENS LAST LETTER—Thus, in a hotel room near the Trenton death house last night, his faithful wife, Anna, began her farewell letter to the doomed carpenter. Before her are the portraits of her husband, in whom she never lost faith, and of their child, Mannfred, for whom Hauptmann so often expressed deep concern. Tragically erect, she stares at a blank wall as she pauses for reassuring words for this painful message. Tears fill her eyes as thoughts, perhaps of happy years gone by, perhaps of bleak years to come, flash through her mind. *International News Photo*

As a Hearst photographer captures the moment, Anna Hauptmann pens her "last message to Bruno." Until her own death some sixty years later, she would protest her husband's innocence. "God knows he did not commit this terrible crime," she insisted in 1992, when the last of her appeals was denied.

Then there was the possible involvement of one or more accomplices consistently described as being "Italian." In a phone conversation with Cemetery John prior to their rendezvous at Woodlawn Cemetery, Dr. Condon had distinctly heard somebody shout in Italian in the background. Later, a man described as medium-sized and Italian had evidently operated as a lookout during the meeting. A few days later, with negotiations stalled, a couple of peddlars—a young man selling needles, the other a scissors grinder—showed up at Condon's doorstep an hour apart. Each left the neighborhood without soliciting any other house on the block, strange behavior that boosted suspicions that they were accomplices casing his place for the presence of police.

If the crime was a conspiracy, in the end nobody other than Bruno Richard Hauptmann was ever brought to justice. After all these years, it seems certain that nobody else ever will be.

Following two last-minute stays of execution, Hauptmann was electrocuted on the morning of April 3, 1936, inside the state prison at Trenton. He maintained his innocence to the very end, despite a newspaper's offer that would have given his family $100,000 in exchange for his confession.

Soon after Hauptmann's execution, the American Bar Association moved to prevent future spectacles by adopting a rule that barred radio and newsreel coverage

Charles, Anne, and three-year-old Jon in 1935: caught in the media glare.

inside the courtroom. The prohibition was broadened in 1952 to include television. By the 1970s, however, the ban fell apart as more than twenty states relaxed restrictions in view of the public's right to know. In 1995, the controversy was revisited when broadcast coverage of the O. J. Simpson murder trial created a new exemplar of the modern media carnival, one that surpassed even the excesses of those six weeks in Flemington.

• • •

The Hauptmann trial gave a perverse twist to Charles's fame. From here on out, more people would associate his name with the kidnap-murder of his son than with the epochal flight that had brought him the kind of attention that made him a target in the first place. Today, cultural references to the kidnapping far outnumber those to the *Spirit of St. Louis.* Sanitized by time of any of the attendant barbarism or sordidness, they blithely pop up on screen, in print, and in casual conversation. "I'm the Lindbergh baby—wah! wah! wah!" said a cartoon character in an episode of the television series *The Simpsons.* "I'm Anne Morrow Lindbergh," announced an actor strutting around in a pink dress and boa in the Robin Williams movie *The Fisher King;* "Where's my baaaby?" Kenneth Starr's wide-ranging investigation of President Bill Clinton caused Democratic counsel Abbe Lowell to joke that the special investigator "doesn't rule out the possibility that the president kidnapped the Lindbergh baby." About the same time, an ESPN producer responded to a suggestion that the network had "dumbed down" sports by wisecracking, "They haven't pinned the Lindbergh kidnapping on us yet." And so on.

Nearly as prevalent are the fantastic theories concerning Lindbergh's "lost son." "There have been a number of people . . . who believe that the baby survived, somehow," wrote Lindbergh's youngest child, Reeve, in her 1998 memoir, *Under A Wing:*

> —a mysterious switch with another child, a Mafia plot, a secret, unfathomably complicated series of misfortunes that resulted in the "real" Lindbergh baby growing up in the wrong family, in California, or in Connecticut, or in Maine, or even, in one case, in Bombay. . . .
>
> I get letters about the kidnapping from about a half dozen different people each year, some claiming to be my last brother, others to be the child of my brother, and to have heard him confess his identity on his deathbed.

As distressing as these breezy references and ersatz Lindbergh offspring are to surviving members of the family, they pale when compared to the wretched public preoccupation with Charles, Anne, and Jon that continued in the wake of Hauptmann's conviction. The masses, it seemed, were unwilling to let go of the sensation of "the crime of the century" or the spectacle of the ensuing "trial of the century." The Lindberghs, hoping to rebuild their lives, contended with crank mail that demanded money and threatened the life of their second child, and fought off press photographers who went so far as to hide outside Jon's nursery school in order to get pictures of the three-year-old. On one infamous occasion, a teacher was driving the boy home when a second car forced them off the road. As Jon cried, a photographer rushed up and snapped a picture.

Charles could no longer tolerate such terrorism in the name of freedom of the press. In December 1935, he quietly made arrangements for his family on the *American Importer.* They were the only passengers. The ship had been out to sea for several hours when the public learned that the object of its obsession had fled. The Lindberghs were headed for England, a land of law and order. Nobody, not even the exiles, knew when they might return.

SOL KARROW

"There were bucks to be made"

To the outside world, the big story coming out of Flemington, New Jersey, in early 1935 was the trial of Bruno Richard Hauptmann for the kidnap-murder of the Lindbergh baby. To the residents of Flemington, the real story was the unprecedented influx of reporters, vendors and tourists to their sleepy hamlet. As longtime Flemington tailor Sol Karrow remembered, the locals were able to turn the pandemonium to their advantage.

Flemington is the county seat of Hunterdon County, so that's why the Hauptmann trial was held here. There might have been some people who didn't want to see all this commotion come to town, but they didn't say much about it. I think everybody—I hate to use the word *enjoyed* it—but they were attracted by the excitement. You don't get too many instances of that in Flemington.

I was born in New York in 1917 and our family moved here in 1923. My dad, Ben Karrow, worked for a very fine couturiere— she had accounts like Mary Pickford—and he wanted to get out of the city. We'd come out to Flemington the year before, one of those week-in-the-country deals, and he liked the environment so much he thought it'd be nice for the family. My sister had just been born. So he came out and started this little tailor shop.

Flemington was a wonderful little town. A very quiet place. We're only twenty-one miles from Trenton, the capital. At that time it was all rural with farms on the outside of town. It only got active when the chicken farmers came in to shop. About that time there

"You couldn't see the sky for the telegraph wires."

were about 2,800 people. Nothing at all like it is today.

It's funny, looking back, but Lindbergh's flight didn't really impress me as a kid. We were aware of it, sure. But I recall a couple of years later, when I was in sixth grade, the teacher said to us, "Write down who your hero is." At that time I was so engrossed in baseball, I put down Ty Cobb as my hero. My teacher read off everybody's heroes and she said, "Isn't it odd? Two years ago Charles Lindbergh crossed the Atlantic and was the biggest hero

in the world, and yet not a single person in this class mentioned his name."

When Lindbergh got married, at this point we were more aware of his importance. Anne Morrow came from Englewood, which was not too far from where we lived. Her father was the ambassador to Mexico, so we were aware of the importance of that family.

The fact that their baby was kidnapped was a sad thing, but I don't think it made much of an impression on me and my friends. It didn't hit us that hard because

Sol Karrow in 1935.

we were still young. We had a state police barracks in town, so we were aware of the activity in trying to find the perpetrator. One of my most vivid memories was when they found the baby's body. In those days we had three papers a day—morning, afternoon, and evening editions. So we would get three different newspapers each day. We had extras coming out. We always hung around the news stand, so we'd get a bunch of papers and sell them.

I guess the only way to describe the trial is to say that you had to be here to believe it. Here you are, in a little town fifty miles from New York and fifty miles from Philadelphia, and suddenly it seems the whole world is invading.

You had all these reporters and telegraph operators. Phones weren't as sophisticated or plentiful, so everything was done by either Western Union or postal telegram. You had this mass of communication—radio people—coming in. You'd look up at the roof of the courthouse, you couldn't see the sky for the telegraph wires. We had some extremely heavy snowfalls during the trial. Of course, in those days you didn't have the kind of sophisticated snow-removing equipment you have today. The only roads that were open were from New York to Flemington and from Trenton to Flemington. The state had to keep them open just to keep communications going.

The Union Hotel in town could not hold this mass of newcomers. So the hotel became like a booking agency. They would rent rooms in private residences. That was a bonanza for everybody. Our apartment was over the store on Main Street. Things weren't very good in those days, so my mother rented one room to three telegraph operators. Probably got a hundred bucks a week. I remember one night when they had an all-night poker game and the place was full of cigarette smoke. They gave my mom an extra couple bucks for the inconvenience. This was not unusual. For all of that, they were a well-behaved group. They were gentlemen. There were no problems.

It was an exciting time. Streets were crowded. We loved it. And why not? You'd see all these famous people coming and going. A couple of kids my age, they'd get souvenir books with autographs and sell them. Everybody was involved in some kind of racket. Some people made these little ladders of tongue depressers and sold them for a couple bucks. Everybody was into something. I mean, there were bucks to be made. In 1935, a couple dimes was a pretty big deal.

I remember a couple of years earlier, there had been a trial in Flemington, where some rich soci-

Damon Runyon was just one of many household names covering the trial.

Sol Karrow today: "You had to be there to believe it."

ety dame had been scammed out of her money. It was summer and the courthouse was not air conditioned. A couple of us kids, before the court would open, would scarf a bunch of cups out of the cup dispenser and sell cold drinks for a dime apiece.

When the Hauptmann trial started I'd already been out of high school a year. My father had asked me to spend a year at the store and help him out—a temporary position, by the way, that lasted fifty-nine years. Anyway, my big job during the trial was to pick up and deliver suits, kind of a valet service. Everybody around these parts knew us. At that time we were the only game in town. If you wanted something pressed, call

Karrow's. So they'd call us up and we'd pick it up and deliver.

So that was my exposure. There was Jim Kilgallen and Dorothy Kilgallen and Adela Rogers St. Johns, all the big hitters from the Hearst group. You had Joe Alsop from the *Herald Tribune,* Arthur Brisbane from the *New York Mirror.* Walter Winchell was here. It was these kinds of bylines that we would handle at the shop.

The one customer that sticks out in my mind is Damon Runyon. I remember the quality of his suits. They were strictly hand-tailored. They were so soft and well-made you could just fold them in your hand. In one of his suit pockets he had a beautiful hand-

kerchief embroidered with his signature. Very foolishly I had it pressed and put in an envelope and returned to him. I always regretted not keeping it because it was such a beautiful thing.

The trial was supposed to last only six or eight days and it wound up lasting two months. It got to the point where these people needed clothes, so my father started taking in men's clothing. That really put us in the clothing business—you know, from just cleaning them to making them.

I went to the trial four or five times. You'd get a pass from the sheriff's office. It'd be good for one session; there was a morning and an afternoon session. You could scalp them, if you wanted to. I don't know what the going price was. Pop went up there himself three or four times. They had a very small mezzanine in the back that didn't hold that many. The courthouse wasn't that large, at least not for this purpose. I remember Lindbergh was stolid, no emotion. Same with Hauptmann. Sitting maybe twenty feet apart. It was hard to tell who the defendant was.

I was intrigued. Oh sure. Especially by the machinations of the prosecution and the defense. The first thing that struck you was the difference between David Wilentz and Edward J. Reilly, the attorneys for the two sides. My impression of Reilly was of a big, pompous city slicker who was going to show these country bumpkins how things ran. He was a syphilitic drunk. He always came in half bombed. I think he did more to hurt than help Hauptmann. A member of the defense team was Lloyd Fisher, who was local. Fisher knew everybody in the county, and if they'd left it up to him to pick the jury

and handle certain parts of the defense, I'm sure he could've gotten Hauptmann off. To his dying day, Fisher always claimed Hauptmann was innocent. Fisher later became my next-door neighbor, and he and I would get into some arguments about that.

A lot of people have tried to compare this trial with the O. J. Simpson trial. They were both media circuses. If there had been television and 24-hour cable shows back then, we would've had to put barriers into town to keep everybody out. But listen, there was only one Lindbergh. One was a true hero, the other was just a professional football player. There's been thousands of those. Another thing: the prosecutors in the Simpson trial made the decision not to seek the death penalty. That wasn't the case with Hauptmann. He was on trial for his life.

I think they got the right man. I've talked with some of the state police involved. I became close with several of them. I'd ask, "Is there any chance that Hauptmann

wasn't guilty?" And they'd say, "No, Sol. There was evidence we didn't even have to use." And that was the general impression among police and detectives.

Hauptmann deserved to be electrocuted. It's only been in the last couple years that I've begun to think that he had to have had some help: the nursemaid, Betty Gow, and Isador Fisch, who fled to Germany. There were probably others that got away.

There aren't too many of us left who remember that time. I think there's one juror left, and a couple of the state police left, but that's about it. Those jurors must have taken a vow of silence, because as far as I know there's never been a single one who's ever made any kind of a comment about the case.

It was such a crazy period. Like I said, you had to see it to believe it. So many different characters.

The excitement lasted seven weeks, then they all pulled up stakes and left. And that was it. Then Flemington went back to its nice, quiet existence.

Lindbergh with Erhard Milch, Hermann Göring's top assistant, during one of the six visits he made to Nazi Germany between 1936 and 1939.

CHAPTER SEVEN

War of Words

A merica's greatest living icon arrived in Liverpool, England, on the last day of 1935, wife and child in tow. The Lindberghs' abrupt departure from the states got the press naturally—and somewhat hypocritically—deploring a national culture so decrepit that it could drive one of its most prominent families into exile overseas. Representative was an editorial in the *New York Herald Tribune*, which lamented that the Lindberghs' quest for "a more tolerable home" in a more civilized country was "its own commentary upon the American social scene."

> Nations have exiled their heroes before; they have broken them with meanness. But when has a nation made life unbearable to one of its most distinguished men through a sheer inability to protect him from its criminals and lunatics and the vast vulgarity of its sensationalists, publicity-seekers . . . and yellow newspapers? It seems as incredible as it is shocking.

The Lindberghs would find a welcoming peace overseas, living first in rural England, then on a small island off the French coast. For the most part, the press obligingly left them alone until their permanent return to the states three years later. This period of personal tranquility, however, was framed in black borders. Europe was on the cusp of a great cataclysm, one that threatened to drag a new generation of Americans into the bloody business of Old World geopolitics. Asia, too, was in upheaval. "By the summer of 1938," Charles later wrote, "no day passed without thoughts and talk of war. Nothing seemed of much importance, after a time, in contrast to the holocaust that would result from a conflict between modern powers."

• • •

While in England, Charles and Anne rented a rambling cottage called Long Barn in the southeast part of the country. Their well-connected landlords were Harold Nicholson and his wife, the writer Vita Sackville-West. Parts of the cottage dated to the fourteenth century, but to the new tenants the inconveniences were offset by its eccentric charms. Anne set about domesticating Long Barn and working on *Listen! The Wind*, an account of their 1933 survey trip that would become a bestseller when published five years later. Meanwhile, her husband pondered the future.

"Charles says he has to make up his mind whether to devote himself to science and mechanics or whether to use his own legend to clean up American politics,"

Exiles: the Lindberghs arrive in England on December 31, 1935.

Nicholson observed in his diary. "He has evidently thought about it a great deal, and thought that on the whole he must follow 'the bent of my mother's family rather than the bent of my father, and follow mechanics and not politics.'" That proved easier said than done.

Charles and Anne regularly explored the continent, typically flying to destinations in a custom-built Miles "Mohawk" monoplane. The sporty two-passenger craft, which had a cruising speed of 170 miles per hour and a range of 1,000 miles, was painted orange and black and featured a sliding glass roof. In the summer of 1936 they used it to visit Nazi Germany for the first time.

The trip, one of several Lindbergh would make to Germany over the next two years, was at the request of Major Truman Smith, the military attaché to the American Embassy in Berlin. The U.S. government was interested in finding out what it could of Germany's air strength, which had increased dramatically during Adolf Hitler's rise to power.

Anne, Jon, and dogs Skean and Thor in front of their home in England, Long Barn.

The Lindberghs at Berlin's Templehof Field on October 11, 1938. The occasion was the International Air Congress.

The Lindberghs flew into Berlin on July 22, 1936, and were treated like royalty at a series of social events. Although he was a civilian, Charles was granted unprecedented access by the Air Ministry, which recognized the famous aviator's visit as a propaganda coup. For a week he toured bases, factories, and laboratories, meeting with pilots, technicians, and scientists. He came away impressed not only by the surprisingly advanced state of German aeronautical design and engineering, but by such portentous sights as the mass production of the Junkers 86 medium bomber and the Junkers 87 Stuka dive bomber.

"We who are in aviation carry a heavy responsibility on our shoulders," he told a roomful of aviators and diplomats at a Berlin luncheon held in his honor, "for while we have have been drawing the world closer together in peace we have stripped the armor of every nation in war. . . . Our libraries, our museums, every institution we value most, are laid bare to our bombardment." Lindbergh's words were widely published, boosting his image as a world citizen. Although the speech could be interpreted as being vaguely critical of Germany's military build-up, top Nazis were not entirely displeased, for it provided a subtle reminder to the rest of the world of the Luftwaffe's lethal potential.

The Lindberghs spent some private time with Herman Göring during an elaborate state luncheon at the air minister's official residence. Göring, second only to Hitler in the Nazi hierarchy, was vain and addicted to pomp, fine food, and morphine, but certain aspects of his character appealed to Charles. Göring, after all, had been a highly decorated combat pilot during the last war, downing twenty-two Allied aircraft and earning the Iron Cross First Class as a member of Richthofen's famous Flying Circus. Like Lindbergh, he had taken a turn on the barnstorming circuit in the 1920s. Appointed Reich Master of the Hunt and Master of the Forest, just two of the many

Touring Hermann Göring's study.

titles and honors Hitler showered upon his most loyal devotee, Göring was an avid outdoorsman and an ardent conservationist, throwing his ballooning weight behind programs to protect such endangered species as the falcon and the eagle. He also knew a great deal about the culture and customs of Charles's ancestral land, having eloped with the wife of a Swedish nobleman.

Charles and Anne joined the number-two Nazi in his box at the opening ceremonies of the Olympic Games. The sporting spectacle allowed the Germans to show off to the world a new society under the swastika, one that was more orderly, more virile. The Lindberghs revealed a grudging admiration of Hitler, an impression shared by many other foreigners dazzled by Germany's remarkable comeback from its recent dark and chaotic past. Even for German citizens, it was easy to overlook the loss of basic freedoms—the elimination of free speech, the outlawing of trade unions, the banning of rival political parties—in the rush to recreate a proud and powerful nation. *Der Fuhrer*'s spellbinding oratory drowned out the weak cries of the Jews, Communists, and intellectuals being persecuted at his direction. Three months before the Lindberghs' visit, the newly bellicose Germans had reoccupied the demilitarized Rhineland in violation of the Treaty of Versailles. England and France did nothing to contest this reckless act of aggression, further emboldening Hitler. Although Charles wasn't blind to the Nazis' menace, he rationalized that the gangster regime was a bulwark against what many observers considered to be the true threat to European civilization, Russia. Charles visited the Soviet Union on three separate occasions during the 1930s, witnessing first-hand the malaise, poverty, and inefficiency of the

Communist system. In his mind Fascists like Hitler and Italy's sawdust Caesar, Benito Mussolini, were preferable to Joseph Stalin, whose purges had killed tens of millions of people since the 1917 revolution.

Upon the Lindberghs' return to England, Charles passed on his impressions to Truman Smith, as well as to Harold Nicholson and members of the British government. In each instance he warned that Germany was putting together the most powerful air force in the world, though time would show that he had grossly overestimated the Luftwaffe's strength and production capacity.

In early 1937, Charles and Anne—then several months pregnant—undertook an arduous three-month trip to India and back. Seeing firsthand the poverty and despair of such hellholes as Calcutta was enervating, but visiting the ruins of ancient Athens during a stopover in Greece produced an apocalyptic vision in Charles. He mused over "how easily strength was perverted to decay" and compared the current tensions in Europe and Asia (where Japan was preparing an all-out invasion of China) to the mutually destructive wars of the past, conflicts that had toppled great civilizations. "War! War!" he lamented. "What useless conflicts there had been through those intervening centuries! Yet one could see no end."

Not long after Charles's epiphanic soul-searching amidst Grecian rubble, German dive-bombers leveled the Spanish Basque town of Guernica in support of General Francisco Franco's Fascists, then embroiled in a devastating civil war with Republican Loyalists. Civilian massacres were becoming sickingly commonplace around the globe. But in the spring of 1937, the indiscriminate slaughter of more than a thousand men, women and children from a new direction—the air—was novel enough to impel Pablo Picasso to paint his most famous work, *Guernica*. The Nazi high command was unmoved by this or any other expressions of outrage over the atrocity; Göring later admitted that he welcomed the opportunity to test the Luftwaffe's bombing capabilities.

As the world continued to slowly unravel, the Lindberghs anticipated the arrival of a new child. On May 12, 1937, the day of King George VI's coronation at Westminster Abbey, Anne gave birth to a third son. The infant was given the unusual name of Land, to honor the maternal side of Charles's family. That fall Charles revisited Germany, handling the controls of a Messerschmitt 109 single-engine fighter and marveling over an experimental helicopter. Once again he reported his findings to Truman Smith. Then, in late November, he and Anne boarded the S.S. *President Harding* for their first trip to the states since leaving for England two years earlier. They spent a frenetic three months at Next Day Hill getting reacquainted with family, friends, and business associates before returning to Long Barn in March 1938. That month, German troops goose-stepped into Austria. The *Anschluss* made seven million German-speaking Austrians citizens of the Greater Reich.

Lindbergh may have disapproved of the forced nature of Austria's annexation, but he did share Hitler's fascination with social engineering and a belief in the genetic primacy of certain groups. His views on eugenics were heavily influenced by his close association with Dr. Alexis Carrel, with whom he was collaborating on a book, *The Culture of Organs*. Carrel was many things to Lindbergh—intellectual mentor, scientific partner, surrogate father—and in the summer of 1938 neighbor was added to the list.

The Lindberghs bought Illiec, a private island off the Brittany coast, in 1938.

Carrel and his wife owned a summer home on Ile Saint-Gildas. Charles never tired of making the inconvenient trips from Long Barn to the rugged, remote islet off the coast of Brittany. When he learned that an adjoining property was up for sale, he immediately bought it for $16,000. The rocky four-acre site, Illiec, was isolated, impractical, but magnificent, "a part of the sea—like a boat in the storm," he wrote. Charles could move between Illiec and Saint-Gildas in a few minutes by boat or, when the tide was low, on foot. The family, along with a caretaker and a cook, moved into the three-story, turreted stone house that had been built on the property in the 1860s. It lacked electricity, plumbing, and heating, creating a back-to-nature experience that was both exhilirating and exasperating. As Anne noted, "the 'simple' life that many men extol . . . is extremely complicated for women." But she, too, appreciated its wild beauty.

The primordial setting suited the nature of Lindbergh's and Carrel's work, for *The Culture of Organs*, published towards the end of 1938, had a Frankenstein-like feel to it. The authors envisioned a day when diseased organs could be removed and repaired as easily as a mechanic using reconditioned parts to overhaul an engine. They predicted a future in which human beings could be frozen and thawed out on demand and organs manipulated in ways that would create a superior species.

Crackpot or visionary? The directors of the Rockefeller Institute had already made up their minds about the controversial doctor with the famous layman assistant. They decided to discontinue their longtime support of Carrel's research. The stated excuse was that Carrel was about to reach the mandatory retirement age of sixty-five, a newly imposed policy. The real reason was that the doctor had become an embarrassment.

A couple of years earlier Carrel had expressed his sensational racial theories and suggestions in a best-selling book, *Man, the Unknown*. Carrel scoffed at the notion that all men were created equal—a fallacy advanced by democracies, he said—and attributed the superiority of the Scandinavians and other white northern races to weak "atmospheric luminosity." Conversely, Carrel explained, the "lower races generally inhabit countries where light is violent and temperature equal and warm." He offered ideas on how the human race might be strengthened, most of which involved brutish dealings with the "unfit and the defective." He advocated selective breeding, the forced sterilization of the socially undesirable, and the "conditioning of petty criminals with the whip." As for murderers, kidnappers, rapists, and armed robbers, they "should be humanely and economically disposed of in small euthanistic institutions supplied with proper gases." He added that a "similar treatment could be advantageously applied to the insane, guilty of criminal acts." As harsh as these procedures

Three generations of Morrows gather at Next Day Hill on May 29, 1939, shortly after the Lindberghs' return from Europe. From left: Jon, Anne, and Land Lindbergh; Anne's mother, Betty Morrow; and Anne's sister Constance and sister-in-law Margot, with their infant sons.

seemed on an individual basis, they were necessary for the greater good of mankind. "Modern society should not hesitate to organize itself with reference to the normal individual," he insisted. There was no room for "philosophical systems and sentimental prejudices" in such proceedings.

Lindbergh did not endorse everything the cranky ideologue wrote or said, but he agreed with a good deal of it. Moreover, Carrel's coldly analytical approach to the mysteries of life and death and his willingness to boldly state and unflinchingly defend his opinions greatly impressed Lindbergh. He certainly was in complete agreement with Carrel's conviction that democratic nations had become flabby and decadent. The British, in particular, struck Charles as too complacent and self-deluded, especially when compared to the energetic Germans. How could England ever hope to win a war with Germany, should it come down to that?

To his satisfaction, Lady Nancy Astor, the celebrated American-born society hostess and the first woman member of Parliament, was pro-appeasement, as was most of her circle. "I was encouraged about the feeling of most of the people there in regard to Germany," Charles observed after a social gathering at Cliveden, Astor's country estate, shortly before the move to Illiec. "They understand the situation better than most Englishmen do these days."

Throughout the summer of 1938, Hitler stridently demanded that Czechoslovakia cede the Sudetenland, with its "oppressed" German population. Winston Churchill, the bane of the "Cliveden set," called for an alliance of nations to stop Germany before it got too strong. Meanwhile, British Prime Minister Neville Chamberlain and French Premier Edouard Daladier anxiously searched for a diplomatic solution.

The Lindberghs, with the blessings of the White House, undertook an inspection tour of Russia, Czechoslovakia, and France during that turbulent summer. Nothing Charles saw of each country's aviation industry changed his opinion that Germany, principally because of the Luftwaffe, held the trump card in the mounting crisis. He related his impressions to already gloomy British, French, and American officials. Germany, he warned, "now has the means of destroying London, Paris, and Prague if she wants to do so. England and France together have not enough modern war planes for effective defence or counter-attack. . . . I am convinced that it is wiser to permit Germany's eastward expansion than to throw England and France, unprepared, into a war at this time." His words were circulated at the very top level of each government.

With all of Western Europe mobilizing, Chamberlain, Daladier, Hitler, and Mussolini met in Munich in a last-ditch effort to avoid war. On September 30, the leaders emerged with a signed agreement that, without Czechoslovakia's input, gave Hitler everything that he demanded. Chamberlain triumphantly declared "peace with honor . . . peace for our time." Churchill knew better. "Britain and France had to choose between war and dishonor," he said of the two nations' abandonment of an ally. "They chose dishonor. They will have war."

Charles would always insist that his influence on the Munich accord was grossly overstated, but there's no denying that his firsthand observations were a factor in the decision-making process that resulted in Europe bowing to a bully. As Hitler would later admit, a united show of force at this point would have called his bluff and forced him to back down from his demands. Although Germany was working mightily to arm itself, in September 1938 it simply did not have the military superiority that Lindbergh described. According to his estimates, the Germans were producing between 500 and 800 planes a month and were capable of building 20,000 a year. In actuality, those production figures were long-range goals; they would not be reached for another four years. The bottom line is that Lindbergh's inflated estimates helped Hitler intimidate Chamberlain and Daladier.

Charles made several more trips to Germany. He admired most of what he saw in the bustling technocracy and seriously considered finding a residence in Berlin. On October 18, 1938, while attending the Lilienthal Society's Aeronautic Congress, he was part of a distinguished international group of diplomats and aviation figures invited to a stag dinner at the American Embassy. At one point that evening, Hermann Göring suddenly approached Lindbergh and, without warning, pulled a medal out of a red leather box. *Der Oceanflieger* was being presented with the *Verdienstkreuz Deutscher Adler* for his lifetime contributions to aviation. The Service Cross of the German Eagle was a handsome medal—a golden cross with four swastikas, strung on a tricolored ribbon—but Lindbergh gave the decoration and its accompanying proclamation, signed by Hitler, little consideration. He'd been given hundreds of such awards in countless ceremonies over the years.

Three weeks later, as the Lindberghs were preparing to move from Illiec to a house in the Berlin suburb of Wannsee, Germany erupted in a nationwide pogrom that came to be known as *Kristallnacht,* "the night of broken glass." Hundreds of Jewish businesses and synagogues were destroyed, tens of thousands of Jews were hauled off to camps, and dozens of people were killed. Suddenly Lindbergh's medal took on greater significance. Many wondered why he refused to symbolically return it

Charles with sons Land and Jon at Lloyd Neck, Long Island, in 1940.

or to publicly denounce the Third Reich. It was pointed out that the only other American to have received the Service Cross was Henry Ford, whose anti-Semitic writings had been avidly read by Hitler while in prison in the 1920s. The press questioned his impending move to Berlin. "There is a good deal of ill feeling towards you," Dr. Carrel wrote Charles as the Lindberghs, shaken by events, opted to settle in Paris instead for the winter.

Charles pondered his next move. He decided that, after more than three years abroad, he could accomplish the most good by returning to America and arguing for a policy of "strength and neutrality."

In April 1939, as Hitler continued his string of broken promises by seizing control of the rest of Czechoslovakia, Lindbergh sailed for the states alone. It was a familiar scene upon arrival, the returning exile running a gauntlet of 150 reporters and photographers as he fled down the *Aquitania*'s gangplank. Anne and the children arrived a few days later. Their disembarkation was made considerably smoother by a guard of one hundred policemen.

On April 20, Charles met privately with President Franklin Roosevelt at the White House, his firsthand observations eagerly sought by his commander in chief. Charles came away from his first meeting with Roosevelt impressed by the man's political skills and personal charm. Although he was anxious to assist in any way possible, he also had a nagging feeling of distrust. The president was "a little too suave, too pleasant, too easy," he remembered.

Anne wrote three best-selling books prior to World War II, with the most controversial being 1940's *The Wave of the Future*. Critics branded her as an appeaser and a defeatist, charges already being leveled at her husband.

The two strong-willed men had butted heads a few years before. In February 1934, the president impulsively revoked all government air mail contracts with private carriers, the result of an investigation that suggested some contracts had been awarded as Republican payoffs. Roosevelt ordered the Army to take over the routes. It proved to be a drastic and deadly move on FDR's part, as several Army pilots were killed flying the mail before the administration was forced to hurriedly open a new round of bidding from commercial airlines. Throughout the controversy, Lindbergh vociferously defended the integrity of Transcontinental & Western Air (which reorganized as Trans World Airlines in order to be eligible for a new contract). Charles emerged with his reputation enhanced, while FDR suffered one of his first public relations defeats as president.

As Anne and the children settled into a new rental house in Lloyd Neck, overlooking Long Island Sound, Lindbergh spent the next several months touring U.S. aviation factories and research facilities. Roosevelt took his recommendations to heart, asking Congress for $300 million to expand the country's Army and Navy air corps into a more modern force.

Meanwhile, Europe was ready to explode. On September 1, 1939, Germany invaded Poland. The attack forced England and France, which had pledged "total and unqualified support" for the Poles, to finally stand up to Hitler. The sequel to the slaughter of 1914–18 was underway.

• • •

Despite his distaste for public life, over the next two years Lindbergh would make it his mission to keep America out of foreign entanglements. He would use the clout of his famous name, employing the very same media that he professed to despise. To appear as neutral as possible, he paid all of his own expenses and rejected all attempts to draft him onto any political ticket.

Unlike many of his fellow noninterventionists, he was not a pacifist; he simply viewed a European war as "racial suicide by internal conflict." In his first radio address, aired from a Washington studio on September 15, 1939, he warned the listeners of the three national networks that "these wars in Europe are not wars in which our civilization is defending itself against some Asiatic intruder. There is no Genghis Khan or Xerxes marching against our Western nations. This is not a question of banding together to defend the White race against foreign invasion. This is simply one more of those age-old quarrels within our own family of nations—a quarrel arising from the errors of the last war—from the failure of the victors of that war to follow a consistent policy of fairness or of force."

In pieces written for mass-circulation magazines he argued that a strong Germany was essential, not only to keep Bolshevism in check but to "dam the Asiatic hordes" that lay beyond. In private he reiterated his fear of "a war which will reduce the strength and destroy the treasures of the White race," a war which might cause the end of Western civilization and pave the way for domination by people of other colors.

Lindbergh's views drew legions of admirers and attracted a like number of critics. To many of the latter, his choice of language was unsettling. Some heard the echoes of his mentor, Dr. Carrel, or detected the traces of Nazi dogma. Allegations that he was a Fascist stung Charles, who thought more deeply about life in all of its complexities than most people. However, for all of his scientific and intellectual probing of eugenics, his carefully examined beliefs often seemed indistinguishable from the knee-jerk opinions of the casual everyday bigot. Like anyone else, his reasoning was shaped by his environment, albeit a highly unique environment. As one of his most capable biographers, A. Scott Berg, pointed out, the high-flying globetrotter had acquired an "Olympian view of the earth," one in which "populations of continents appeared to him as masses of people." His chronic inability to connect with most individuals on an intimate level reinforced his xenophobic view of the world.

His refusal to return the Service Cross of the German Eagle contributed to the growing public hostility. He regarded the uproar surrounding it as a "teapot tempest" and felt that if the flap over the medal didn't exist, his opponents would have manufactured some other controversy. Columnist Walter Lippmann, a close friend of Anne's father, privately referred to Lindbergh as "a Nazi lover." Vita Sackville-West called Charles "a shit" in letters to her husband, who offered some dimestore psychoanalysis. In the fall of 1939, Harold Nicholson wrote an article for the *British Spectator* (subsequently reprinted in the *New York Times*) attributing what he perceived to be the sea change in Charles's personality to the kidnap-murder of his son. "The suffering which the dreadful crime entailed upon himself and those he loved pierced his armor. He identified the outrage to his private life first with the popular press and by inevitable association with freedom of speech, and then with freedom. He began to loathe democracy. . . . Let us not allow this incident to blind us to the great qualities of Charles Lindbergh. He is and always will be not merely a schoolboy hero, but a schoolboy."

A schoolboy with remarkable influence, however. As the German *blitzkrieg* of 1939–40 brought most of Europe under the swastika—including an astonishing six-week defeat of France—and Americans argued their proper place in world events, Charles emerged as the country's leading symbol of neutrality. On Sunday, August 4, 1940, at Chicago's Soldier Field, he aired his views in front of a live audience for the first time. The stadium rocked with cheers. The German military attaché in Washington was General Friedrich von Boetticher. In a dispatch written two days after Lindbergh's speech, von Boetticher informed Berlin:

> The forces opposing the Jewish element and the present policy of the
> United States have been mentioned in my reports. . . . The greatly gifted
> Lindbergh, whose connections reach very far, is much the most important
> of them all. The Jewish element and Roosevelt fear the spiritual and, partic-
> ularly, the moral superiority and purity of this man.
> On Sunday Lindbergh delivered a blow that will hurt the Jews.
> He . . . stressed that America should strive for sincere collaboration with
> Germany with a view to peace and the preservation of Western culture. . . .
> The chorus of the Jewish element casting suspicion on Lindbergh in the
> press, and his denunciation . . . as a "fifth columnist," that is, a traitor, mere-
> ly serve to underline the fear of the spiritual power of this man, about whose
> progress I have reported since the beginning of the war and in whose great
> importance for future German-American relations I believe.

As Lindbergh spoke, the Battle of Britain was underway. When the first German planes had crossed the English Channel in July, Göring boasted that it would take the Luftwaffe only four days to gain air superiority. Instead, the Brits baffled Hitler—and Lindbergh—with their resilience and resolve. Within three months the Germans lost 1,733 planes, forcing Hitler to postpone Operation Sea Lion, the anticipated invasion of England. However, the terror raids of civilian targets continued. Neutral America also was bombarded—with magazine and newsreel images of caved-in cathedrals and bandaged infants that troubled the national conscience. Edward R. Murrow, the CBS radio correspondent in London during the blitz, literally became the voice of American involvement. Although he never publicly criticized Lindbergh, in private he once referred to Long Barn as "the house which gave refuge to Charles Lindbergh—now giving refuge to children who had to leave London because of the bombing by Lindbergh's friends!"

Anne, keen to support her husband in a debate that was consuming him, got more than she bargained for with the publication of a slim volume called *The Wave of the Future*. It hit bookstores in October 1940, not long after she had given birth to a daughter, Anne Spencer. Within a month it was heading the best-seller list. In it she argued that the inherent evils of Nazism, Fascism, and Communism were the "scum" of a giant wave of change sweeping over the world. To resist it was fruitless. She cat-alogued the "sins" of the Nazis—"persecution, aggression, war and theft"—and com-pared them with the "sins" of democratic nations like England, France, and the

On October 2, 1940, Anne gave birth to her fourth child and first daughter. The baby, named Anne Spencer, is seen with her mother and brothers Jon and Land on Martha's Vineyard in 1941.

United States: "blindness, selfishness, smugness, lethargy and resistance to change." The best course of action for America was to concentrate on defending its own shores while riding out the wave.

Anne's "confession of faith" was well-received by isolationists and pacifists but incurred the wrath and ridicule of prominent reviewers like Dorothy Thompson and E. B. White. More hurtful was the criticism of valued friends and close relatives who considered her elegantly written work illogical and naive. President Roosevelt, elected to an unprecedented third term that fall, referred to her work in his inaugural address. "There are men who believe that . . . tyranny and slavery have become the surging wave of the future, and that freedom is an ebbing tide," he said. "But we Americans know that this is not true."

Anne was shattered by the negative reaction to what she had intended to be a poetic, contemplative look at the world crisis. By stepping out of the background, the popular author had now become linked with her husband as an appeaser and defeatist by millions of Americans. It would take years for Anne and her literary reputation to recover from the pummeling.

FDR had defeated Wendell Willkie partially on his promise to keep the country out of war. However, by early 1941 he had dubbed America the "arsenal of democracy" and was working to get the highly controversial Lend-Lease Act through Congress. Lindbergh came to Capitol Hill to testify against the bill, which allowed the president to ship war material on credit to any country that he determined was vital to U.S. interests. Its passage marked a major shift from neutrality and bolstered fears of an emerging "American Fuhrer" in the White House. The rancor surrounding lend-lease, coming on the heels of congressional approval of the first peacetime draft in U.S. history, inspired many ordinary citizens worried over the path the country was taking to join a new but influential group.

The Committee to Defend America First had been organized by several Yale University students in the spring of 1940 to promote a policy of "hemisphere defense rather than European intervention." No foreign power would dare attack a *prepared* America, the committee insisted. Although organizers professed to be neither pacifists nor affiliated with any political party, most high-profile America Firsters shared a visceral dislike of FDR and the New Deal's progressive social agenda. These included Senators Robert Taft of Ohio and Burton Wheeler of Montana, *Chicago Tribune* publisher Colonel Robert McCormick, and Sears-Roebuck chairman General Robert Wood, who chaired the national committee of America First. Its ranks also boasted such well-known figures as humorist Irvin S. Cobb, novelist Kathleen Norris, and former flying ace Eddie Rickenbacker. Alice Roosevelt Longworth, the eldest child of Theodore Roosevelt, later admitted that "a great deal" of her involvement in the organization "was entirely mischief and dislike of Franklin . . . anything to annoy Franklin."

In October 1940, Lindbergh accepted an invitation to speak at an America First rally at Yale's Woolsey Hall. He concentrated his half-hour address on the situation in Europe. (He dismissed the growing turmoil in the Orient with the remarkably imprescient observation that "no nation in Asia has developed their aviation sufficiently to be a serious menace to the United States at this time. . . .") The overwhelming reception he got from the 3,000 people on hand convinced him to throw in his lot with what he considered to be the most impressive of the many antiwar groups seeking his support.

Lindbergh would make thirteen America First appearances in all. His involvement attracted supporters across the country and helped raise the organization's membership from 300,000 at the beginning of 1941 to a peak of 800,000 several months later. However, his mother and mother-in-law, both staunchly pro-British, were not among them. Neither were Harry Guggenheim, Dr. Carrel, Henry Breckinridge, and other close friends who chose to keep a social as well as philosophical distance. Charles and Anne were hurt by the ostracism, but they stubbornly stayed the course.

On April 23, 1941, as the seemingly invincible Wehrmacht was hammering out victories in North Africa and the Balkans, and Hitler was secretly preparing to unleash 3 million men on an all-out attack on the Soviet Union, Lindbergh took the podium at New York's Manhattan Center. It was one of the first mass meetings of America First and came at a time when polls showed 80 percent of Americans opposed going to war against Germany. Lindbergh ripped into the British government, which he accused of harboring "one last desperate plan"—to get the U. S. to send another American Expeditionary Force to Europe and "to share with England militarily, as well as financially, the fiasco of this war." He also accused England of encouraging smaller nations to "fight against hopeless odds."

Lindbergh's unwillingness in this or any other speech to directly confront the evils

Lindbergh making his case for American nonintervention during a 1941 speech at Fort Wayne, Indiana.

that were at the black heart of Nazism frustrated many Americans. One of the more deeply disillusioned was correspondent Bill Shirer, who had been in Paris that magic May evening in 1927. "Apparently," Shirer acidly noted in *The Rise and Fall of the Third Reich*, "it did not occur to this man that Yugoslavia and Greece, which Hitler had just crushed, were brutally attacked without provocation, and that they had instinctively tried to defend themselves because they had a sense of honor and because they had courage even in the face of hopeless odds."

The administration, carefully preparing the country for what it saw as an unavoidable confrontation with Germany, felt threatened by Lindbergh's immense popularity among the antiwar faction and took every opportunity to discredit him. During a White House press conference two days after the New York speech, Roosevelt obliquely referred to his antagonist as a "copperhead," an archaic term for a defeatist or traitor. Charles, feeling that his honor was impugned, petulantly struck back. On April 28, he informed the president and the press that he was resigning his commission in the reserves.

"I had hoped that I might exercise my right as an American citizen to place my viewpoint before the people of my country in time of peace without giving up the privilege of serving my country as an Air Corps officer in the event of war," Lindbergh wrote his commander in chief. He took this action "with the utmost regret," he continued, "for my relationship with the Air Corps is one of the things which has meant most to me in my life. I place it second only to my right as a citizen to speak freely to my fellow countrymen. . . . I will continue to serve my country to the best of my ability as private citizen."

Citizen Lindbergh threw his campaign into high gear, even as death threats forced him to move the family into a new house and the FBI began tapping his phones. Over the next several months he attacked the administration in increasingly strident tones, his speeches and articles stressing the immediate need for "new leadership." With the next presidential election more than three years off, Roosevelt's circle interpreted Lindbergh's words as being nothing less than a cry for impeachment. Secretary of the Interior Harold Ickes, Roosevelt's principal mouthpiece, responded by calling Charles the "number one Nazi fellow traveler" and claiming that he was the "first American to raise aloft the standard of pro-Nazism."

Anti-Lindbergh sentiment grew apace. He was attacked in signed editorials and anonymous hate mail. His books were pulled off library shelves. Newsreel images of him often provoked hisses and jeers inside theatres. Even Dr. Seuss—the pen name of illustrator Theodor Seuss Geisel—weighed in against him. In 1941, the author of such children's classics as *The Cat in the Hat* was drawing political cartoons for *PM*, a feisty "popular front" New York tabloid. Geisel regularly lampooned Lindbergh as an ostrich who preferred to keep his head in the sand. He composed a piece of Seussian doggerel that accused the man who had crossed the Atlantic "With fortitude and a ham sandwich" of now shivering "At the sound of the gruff German landgwich."

To a degree Charles was being punished for the sins of others. Several major figures who either belonged to or endorsed America First, including Henry Ford and Father Charles Coughlin, the Catholic "radio priest," were established anti-Semites. Lindbergh was always careful to avoid any contact with fringe groups like the Silver Shirts or the Bund, lest he be associated in the public mind with their racist vitriol. But ultimately he could not contain his own antagonism toward those parties that he had long ago identified in his mind as the principal "war agitators." These included a people for whom he had always expressed ambivalent feelings.

Just a few days before German tanks rumbled across Poland in 1939, Charles had met with a pair of rock-ribbed conservatives, news commentator Fulton Lewis Jr., and former undersecretary of state William R. Castle. They discussed what actions they might take as a group to keep the country out of the impending conflict. Among the points they agreed on was the "effect of the Jewish influence in our press, radio, and motion pictures," Charles told his journal. "I fear that trouble lies ahead in this regard. Whenever the Jewish percentage of total population becomes too high, a reaction seems to invariably occur. It is too bad because a few Jews of the right type are, I believe, an asset to any country, adding to rather than detracting from its strength."

For some time Charles had been threatening to expose "the groups that were most powerful and effective in pushing the United States toward involvement in the war." Now, with a polarized nation on the edge of the abyss, he decided to make good on his threat. The occasion would be an America First speech, scheduled for September 11, 1941, in Des Moines, Iowa.

As always, Anne read the draft of Charles's speech beforehand. This time his words filled her with "black gloom," she said. "We had a terrible row about," she recalled in a *60 Minutes* interview many years later. "I felt terrible and he just didn't believe me about it. . . . I said I think to rouse anti-Semitism in the country is much worse than war. I'd rather have war, but he said, 'That's not what I'm doing.' He simply couldn't see it."

Anne, bracing for the worst, did not accompany her husband to the Des Moines Coliseum. "It is not difficult to understand why Jewish people desire the overthrow of Nazi Germany," Charles told the 8,000 people assembled there.

Spreading the Lovely Goebbels Stuff

Lindbergh's Des Moines speech was branded anti-Semetic by many in the press, including political cartoonist Dr. Seuss.

The persecution they suffered in Germany would be sufficient to make bitter enemies of any race. No person with a sense of the dignity of mankind can condone the persecution of the Jewish race in Germany. But no person of honesty and vision can look on their pro-war policy here today without seeing the dangers involved in such a policy, both for us and for them.

Instead of agitating for war, the Jewish groups in this country should be opposing it in every possible way, for they will be among the first to feel its consequences. Tolerance is a virtue that depends upon peace and strength. History shows that it cannot survive war and devastation. A few far-sighted Jewish people realize this, and stand opposed to intervention. But the majority still do not. Their greatest danger to this country lies in their large ownership and influence in our motion pictures, our press, our radio, and our government.

I am not attacking either the Jewish or the British people. Both races, I admire. But I am saying that the leaders of both the British and Jewish races, for reasons which are understandable from their viewpoint as they are inadvisable from ours, for reasons which are not American, wish to involve us in the war. We cannot blame them for looking out for what they believe to be their own interests, but we must also look out for ours. We cannot allow the natural passions and prejudices of other peoples to lead our country to destruction.

The reaction to Lindbergh's words was a public defrocking. He was excoriated by Jews, Protestants, and Catholics, interventionists and noninterventionists alike. As Anne had feared, critics had not objectively evaluated his message as a whole, but instead seized upon such exclusionary phrases as "not American" and "other peoples" to paint him as a bigot. "The voice is the voice of Lindbergh," said the *San Francisco Chronicle*, "but the words are the words of Hitler." *Liberty* magazine declared him "the most dangerous man in America," while Walter Winchell clucked that Lindbergh's "halo has become his noose."

Moderate members of America First disavowed Lindbergh's remarks and fled the organization, leaving it in the hands of the more hardcore right wingers. "I honestly don't think Lindbergh is an anti-Semite," said Norman Thomas, who disassociated himself and the Socialist party from America First, "but I think he is a great idiot. Not all Jews are for war and Jews have a right to agitate for war if we have a right to agitate against it. . . ." Whatever Lindbergh's true feelings about Jewry—and every person close to the man vigorously insisted he was never an anti-Semite—he was at the very least guilty of poor judgment. Rightly or wrongly, he had now become "the symbol of anti-Semitism in this country," Anne wrote. "One thing I think you have to realize is that he was not a great reader," she added in his defense a few years after his death. "Had he read Goebbels and Hitler and all of them, he would have known that people who really are anti-Semitic start with these statements."

Personal attacks only strengthened his resolve. The self-righteousness that had characterized his father's lost cause against U.S. intervention a quarter-century earlier was evident in his own dismissive attitude toward carpers. Charles, a self-described "stubborn Swede," never once considered returning his Nazi medal. He refused to criticize the Nazi regime, or, for that matter, to praise the doughty British, who had rallied around their new prime minister, Winston Churchill. In the autumn of 1941, with the majority of Americans favoring aid to the embattled Allies but still hoping to stay out of the actual fighting, Lindbergh remained as jut-jawed as the eloquently tenacious Churchill. His convictions continued to draw support among noninterventionists, even after that disastrous evening in Des Moines.

Then, three days before he was to deliver an address in Boston, Japanese warplanes attacked the U.S. fleet at Pearl Harbor. At a stroke, one of the most contentious foreign policy debates in American history was finally and catastrophically settled. Now, Lindbergh told his journal, "I can see nothing to do under these circumstances except to fight."

CHARLES LINDBERGH

"War is not inevitable"

Charles Lindbergh spelled out his logic for opposing American involvement in a foreign war in a series of speeches. The following address was given at an America First rally held in New York on April 23, 1941, and is published here in its entirety.

There are many viewpoints from which the issues of this war can be argued. Some are primarily idealistic. Some are primarily practical. One should, I believe, strive for a balance of both. But, since the subjects that can be covered in a single address are limited, tonight I shall discuss the war from a viewpoint which is primarily practical. It is not that I believe ideals are unimportant, even among the realities of war; but if a nation is to survive in a hostile world, its ideals must be backed by the hard logic of military practicability. If the outcome of war depended upon ideals alone, this would be a different world than it is today.

I know I will be severely criticized by the interventionists in America when I say we should not enter a war unless we have a reasonable chance of winning. That, they will claim, is far too materialistic a viewpoint. They will advance again the same arguments that were used to persuade France to declare war against Germany in 1939. But I do not believe that our American ideals and our way of life will gain through an unsuccessful war. And I know that the United States is not prepared to wage war in Europe successfully at this time.

We are no better prepared today than France was when the interventionists in Europe persuaded her to attack the Siegfried Line.

I have said before and I will say again that I believe it will be a tragedy to the entire world if the British Empire collapses. That is one of the main reasons why I opposed this war before it was declared and why I have constantly advocated a negotiated peace. I did not feel that England and France had a reasonable chance of winning. France has now been defeated; and despite the propaganda and confusion of recent months, it is now obvious that England is losing the war. I believe this is realized even by the British government. But they have one last desperate plan remaining. They hope that they may be able to persuade us to send another American Expeditionary Force to Europe and to share with England militarily as well as financially the fiasco of this war.

I do not blame England for this hope, or for asking for our assistance. But we now know that she declared a war under circumstances which led to the defeat of every nation that sided with her, from Poland to Greece. We know that in the desperation of war England promised to all those nations armed assistance that she could not send. We know that she misinformed them, as she has misinformed us, concerning her state of preparation, her military strength, and the progress of the war.

In time of war, truth is always replaced by propaganda. I do not believe we should be too quick to criticize the actions of a belligerent nation. There is always the question whether we, ourselves, would do better under similar circumstances. But we in this country have a right to think of the welfare of America first, just as the people in England thought first of their own country when they encouraged the smaller nations of Europe to fight against hopeless odds. When England asks us to enter this war, she is considering her own future and that of her Empire. In making our reply, I believe we should consider the future of the United States and that of the Western Hemisphere.

It is not only our right but it is our obligation as American citizens to look at this war objectively and to weigh our chances for success if we should enter it. I have attempted to do this, especially from the standpoint of aviation; and I have been forced to the conclusion that we cannot win this war for England, regardless of how much assistance we extend.

I ask you to look at the map of Europe today and see if you can suggest any way in which we could win this war if we entered it. Suppose we had a large army in America, trained and equipped. Where would we send it to fight? The campaigns of the war show only too clearly how difficult it is to force a landing, or to maintain an army, on a hostile coast.

Suppose we took our Navy from the Pacific and used it to convoy British shipping. That would not win the war for England. It would, at best, permit her to exist under the constant bombing of the German air fleet. Suppose we had an air force that we could send to Europe. Where could it operate? Some of our squadrons might be based in the British Isles, but it is physically impossible to base enough aircraft in the British Isles alone to equal in strength the aircraft that can be based on the continent of Europe.

I have asked these questions on the supposition that we had in existence an army and an air force large enough and well enough equipped to send to Europe; and that we would dare to remove our Navy from the Pacific. Even on this basis, I do not see how we could invade the continent of Europe successfully as long as all of that continent and most of Asia is under Axis domination. But the fact is that none of these suppositions are correct. We have only a one-ocean Navy. Our Army is still untrained and inadequately equipped for foreign war. Our air force is deplorably lacking in

Some of the leading spokespersons for America First in New York City, 1941. From left: Senator Burton K. Wheeler, Lindbergh, novelist Kathleen Norris, and socialist leader Norman Thomas.

modern fighting planes.

When these facts are cited, the interventionists shout that we are defeatists, that we are undermining the principles of democracy, and that we are giving comfort to Germany by talking about our military weakness. But everything I mention here has been published in our newspapers and in the reports of congressional hearings in Washington. Our military position is well known to the governments of Europe and Asia. Why, then, should it not be brought to the attention of our own people?

I say it is the interventionists in America, as it was in England and in France, who give comfort to the enemy. I say it is they who are undermining the principles of democracy when they demand that we take a course to which more than 80 percent of our citizens are opposed. I charge them with being the real defeatists, for

their policy has led to the defeat of every country that followed their advice since this war began. There is no better way to give comfort to an enemy than to divide the people of a nation over the issue of foreign war. There is no shorter road to defeat than by entering a war with inadequate preparation. Every nation that has adopted the interventionist policy of depending on someone else for its own defense has met with nothing but defeat and failure.

When history is written, the responsibility for the downfall of the democracies of Europe will rest squarely upon the shoulders of the interventionists who led their nations into war, uninformed and unprepared. With their shouts of defeatism and their disdain of reality, they have already sent countless thousands of young men to death in Europe. From the campaign of Poland to that of Greece, their prophecies have been false and their policies have failed. Yet these are the people who are calling us defeatists in America today. And they have led this country, too, to the verge of war.

There are many such interventionists in America, but there are more people among us of a different type. That is why you and I are assembled here tonight. There is a policy open to this nation that will lead to success—a policy that leaves us free to follow our own way of life and to develop our own civilization. It is not a new and untried idea. It was advocated by Washington. It was incorporated in the Monroe Doctrine. Under its guidance the United States became the greatest nation in the world.

It is based upon the belief that the security of a nation lies in the strength and character of its own people. It recommends the maintenance of armed forces sufficient to defend this hemisphere from attack by any combination of foreign powers. It demands faith in an independent American destiny. This is the policy of the America First Committee today. It is a policy not of isolation but of independence; not of defeat but of courage. It is a policy that led this nation to success during the most trying years of our history, and it is a policy that will lead us to success again.

We have weakened ourselves for many months, and, still worse, we have divided our own people by this dabbling in Europe's wars. While we should have been concentrating on American defense we have been forced to argue over foreign quarrels. We must turn our eyes and our faith back to our own country before it is too late. And when we do this a different vista opens before us. Practically every difficulty we would face in invading Europe becomes an asset to us in defending America. Our enemy, and not we, would then have the problem of transporting millions of troops across the ocean and landing them on a hostile shore. They, and not we, would have to furnish the convoys to transport guns and trucks and munitions and fuel across 3,000 miles of water. Our battleships and submarines would then be fighting close to their home bases. We would then do the bombing from the air and the torpedoing at sea. And if any part of an enemy convoy should ever pass our Navy and our air force, they would still be faced with the guns of our coast artillery and behind them the divisions of our Army.

The United States is better situated from a military standpoint than any other nation in the world. Even in our present condition of unpreparedness no foreign power is in a position to invade us today. If we concentrate on our own defenses and build the strength that this nation should maintain, no foreign army will ever attempt to land on American shores.

War is not inevitable for this country. Such a claim is defeatism in the true sense. No one can make us fight abroad unless we ourselves are willing to do so. No one will attempt to fight us here if we arm ourselves as a great nation should be armed. Over 100 million people in this nation are opposed to entering the war. If the principles of democracy mean anything at all, that is reason enough for us to stay out. If we are forced into a war against the wishes of an overwhelming majority of our people, we will have proved democracy such a failure at home that there will be little use fighting for it abroad.

The time has come when those of us who believe in an independent American destiny must band together and organize for strength. We have been led toward war by a minority of our people. This minority has power. It has influence. It has a loud voice. But it does not represent the American people.

During the last several years I have traveled over this country from one end to the other. I have talked to many hundreds of men and women, and I have letters from tens of thousands more who feel the same way as you and I. Most of these people have no influence or power. Most of them have no means of expressing their convictions except by their vote, which has always been against this war. They are the citizens who have had to work too hard at their daily jobs to organize political meetings. Hitherto, they have relied upon their vote to express their feelings; but now they find that it is hardly remembered except in the oratory of a political campaign.

These people, the majority of hardworking American citizens, are with us. They are the true strength of our country. And they are beginning to realize, as you and I, that there are times when we must sacrifice our normal interests in life in order to insure the safety and the welfare of our nation.

Such a time has come. Such a crisis is here. That is why the America First Committee has been formed—to give voice to the people who have no newspaper or newsreel or radio station at their command; to the people who must do the paying and the fighting and the dying if this country enters the war.

Whether or not we do enter the war rests upon the shoulders of you in this audience; upon us here on this platform; upon meetings of this kind that are being held by Americans in every section of the United States today. It depends upon the action we take and the courage we show at this time. If you believe in an independent destiny for America, if you believe that this country should not enter the war in Europe, we ask you to join the America First Committee in its stand. We ask you to share our faith in the ability of this nation to defend itself, to develop its own civilization, and to contribute to the progress of mankind in a more constructive and intelligent way than has yet been found by the warring nations of Europe. We need your support, and we need it now. The time to act is here.

Lindbergh serving as a civilian "technical adviser" on Emirau Island, May 1944.

CHAPTER EIGHT

Redemption

Although America First resisted disbanding in the immediate aftermath of Pearl Harbor, the organization formally dissolved with the subsequent declarations of war on the United States by Japan's Axis partners, Germany and Italy. Following the lead of millions of their countrymen, many members either enlisted or got their affairs in order while awaiting the inevitable draft notice. However, getting into the fray proved problematic for the man variously described over the preceding two years as a traitor, appeaser, defeatist, Fascist, Nazi lover, anti-Semite, and fifth columnist. Charles Lindbergh had publicly criticized his commander in chief and made a press event out of resigning his commission. Ever the patriot despite his outspoken views, he now found himself frozen out of serving his country in or out of uniform by a vindictive FDR. The administration made it clear that any company looking to acquire lucrative defense contracts had better not put Lindbergh on the payroll. "I'll clip that young man's wings," said Roosevelt.

But Charles had a powerful friend in Dearborn. Henry Ford was one of the few people who could successfully stand up to Roosevelt. Ford despised FDR and considered his New Deal programs to be nothing more than Bolshevism with a lot of initials. Still, business was business. Ford signed a $200-million contract to build bombers at the huge Willow Run plant west of Detroit. The administration had to tread carefully with the cantankerous industrialist, who on April 3, 1942, hired Lindbergh as a technical consultant.

In addition to the senile Ford, the cast of characters at Willow Run included hard-boiled production chief "Cast Iron" Charlie Sorenson and Harry Bennett, a tatooed thug who oversaw the old man's antiquated notions of labor relations. "Oh, we had some experiences in those days at Ford," Charles recalled. "It was an extraordinary place to work. All kinds of things happening all the time. They even had fist fights among the staff. And Ford himself—a genius, a real genius, and an eccentric, those qualities seem to go together—was extraordinary. There never was a dull moment around him." To Lindbergh's mild astonishment, this crew managed to get the massive plant producing B-24 bombers, though never anywhere near the one-plane-per-hour rate that had been promised. As compensation for his work in conducting test flights and serving as Ford's representative at meetings, Charles asked for only $666.66 a month. The amount was equivalent to what a colonel made in the Air Corps.

The Willow Run bomber plant.

Charles moved the family into a rented house in Bloomfield Hills, an exclusive suburb north of Detroit. The wooded three-acre setting seemed ideal for Anne and the children. Scott, their fifth child, was born at Henry Ford Hospital on August 13, 1942. The new place wasn't without tragedy. Shortly after their arrival in Michigan, one of the Lindberghs' dogs was killed by a passing car on Cranbrook Road. Two weeks later their beloved German shepherd, Thor, who had faithfully guarded the family since being acquired after little Charlie's kidnapping, died quietly of old age under a hickory tree.

Throughout his time with Ford, Lindbergh did his best to stay out of the public eye, turning down interview requests and avoiding potentially embarrassing situations. He purposely avoided meeting Roosevelt when the president showed up to inspect Willow Run, and demonstrated no curiosity at all when British aircraft experts, fresh off the Battle of Britain, visited the next day.

During her nearly three years in Michigan, Anne grew more comfortable with the idea of settling permanently in the area. Eventually she took sculpting classes at the Cranbrook Academy of Art and made friends with several local artists, including sculptor Carl Milles and architect Eero Saarinen. "I'd see Lindbergh every so often. He was a reserved kind of person," said Dominick Vettraino, who headed Cranbrook's security force then. "But Anne was a little more outgoing. Henry Ford gave them a trailer that they parked in the woods behind the house. Anne wrote one of her books in there. I remember helping Lindbergh push the trailer one night. They all kept a low profile. I know a couple of the kids [Jon and Land] went to Brookside Elementary. We were all quite concerned with what had happened in New Jersey, so we and the Bloomfield police always kept an eye out."

Ford's prized employee chafed at being a civilian at war. Now in his forties, and with five dependents to care for, Charles would have been exempt from service even if Roosevelt had not arranged his bystander status. But standing on the sidelines was unacceptable to someone who had grown accustomed to being in the center of events. Groveling for a commission, however, was not an option for Lindbergh.

Instead, he assumed the duties of a lab mouse. In September 1942, he underwent ten days of intensive testing at the aeromedical laboratory at the Mayo Clinic in Rochester, Minnesota. While seated inside a one-man altitude chamber that simulated the cabin pressure

Lindbergh testing the effects of altitude at the Mayo Clinic in September 1942.

of a pilot flying at 40,000 feet, scientists conducted experiments on his temperature and accompanying reactions. Several times he passed out. Charles's recommendations proved vital to coping with the problem of hypoxia, the loss of oxygen in the blood that accompanies high-altitude flying. Afterwards, he put the new P-47 "Thunderbolt" being developed for the Air Force through weeks of tests. On one flight he blacked out at 36,000 feet, coming to only after the single-engined fighter had dropped 20,000 feet into denser air.

Starting at the end of 1942 and continuing until the following July, Charles also performed consulting work for the United Aircraft Corporation in Hartford, Connecticut. There he helped fine-tune the Navy's F4U "Corsair" fighter. The term "top gun" didn't exist then, but if it had the middle-aged legend probably would have qualified, as in maneuvers Charles regularly outperformed fighter jocks half his age.

Charles was invigorated by all the flying and mock combat and seemed downright boyish, observed Anne. But returning to uniform was still out of the question. Then one January day in 1944, Lindbergh stumbled across a way of getting sent to a war zone. During a Washington luncheon with Marine Corps Brigadier General Louis E. Wood, he was asked why he didn't go to the Pacific and check out the performance of the Corsairs that he had helped develop.

"I'm not in the service," Charles said.

"What does that matter?" asked Wood. "Why can't you go as a civilian?"

"The White House would never allow it," replied Charles.

Lindbergh, seen here with Marine fliers and ground crew members on Emirau Island, flew fifty combat missions in the Pacific. Half were flown in single-engine Corsairs (shown), the rest in twin-engine P-38s.

Wood was unimpressed. "Why does the White House have to know?"

By late April Charles was on his way to the front, wearing a Navy officer's uniform, custom-tailored by Brooks Brothers and carrying no rank or insignia. He was officially classified as a "technical representative" of United, which meant that he could go on missions as an observer, but not as a participant.

Once in the war zone, however, the line separating civilian from combatant became blurred. On May 22, 1944, he took off in a Marine Corsair from Green Island, Guadalcanal, part of a four-plane patrol that was to provide support for a raid on Rabaul. They met no Japanese fighters, but on the flight back the Americans strafed enemy installations. Upon landing, Lindbergh was reprimanded by the commanding officer. "You have a right to observe combat as a technician," the marine colonel said, "but not to fire guns." Of course, a fellow pilot interjected, it would be perfectly all right if Lindbergh engaged in a little "target practice" on the way back, wouldn't it? Within a week, the unranked civilian was participating in bombing runs against enemy bases on Kavieng, New Britain, and New Ireland.

Having experienced firsthand the capabilities of the Corsair, Charles wanted to check out the P-38 twin-engined fighters being flown by Army Air Corps pilots. On June 26 he reported to Hollandia, where Colonel Charles MacDonald commanded the 475th Fighter Group. The next morning he was part of a "four-plane anti-boredom flight" to Jefman and Samate. Rounding out this formidable formation were a trio of aces: MacDonald, Major Thomas McGuire, and Lieutenant Colonel Meryl Smith. Despite having previously logged only eight hours of flying time in the P-38, the newcomer performed admirably under fire, sinking an enemy barge. "In the days that followed, Lindbergh was indefatigable," MacDonald wrote later. "He flew more missions than was normally expected of a regular combat pilot. He dive-bombed enemy positions, sank barges and . . . was shot at by almost every anti-aircraft gun the Nips had in western New Guinea."

News of Lindbergh's unauthorized presence in the Southwest Pacific was bound to reach General Douglas MacArthur, who ordered him to his headquarters in Brisbane, Australia. The two had a cordial meeting. MacArthur urged Charles to be careful, to avoid getting his head "chopped off by the Japs," and "caus[ing] us any trouble at home." The supreme commander agreed to let Charles continue to skirt regulations while he taught pilots how to increase their combat radius.

This would become Lindbergh's greatest contribution to the war effort. He demonstrated that a pilot could conserve fuel, and thus significantly extend his plane's range, by lowering the engine's revolutions and raising the manifold pressure. According to General George C. Kenney, who commanded the Allied Air Forces, "When Lindbergh joined us, the P-38s were considered to have a range of 400 miles. Under his training P-38s were able to escort bombers all the way to Balikpapan, Borneo, fight over the target, and get home with a reserve supply of fuel for a 950-mile mission." Kenney credited Lindbergh with moving up the timetable for MacArthur's invasion of the Phillippines, thus shortening the Pacific war by several months and saving thousands of lives.

Lieutenant C. J. Rieman was a pilot with the 433rd Fighter Squadron when Charles showed up the last week of July 1944. As a ten-year-old, the New Jersey native had caught an imperishable glimpse of Lindbergh, perched in the back of a Packard, combing the confetti out of his hair, as New York welcomed its hero back home from Paris. Now he found himself occasionally flying in formation alongside the legend with the receding hairline.

"Our commanding officer told us to address him as 'Mr. Lindbergh,' not 'Colonel,'" recalled Rieman, today a retired funeral home director living in Colorado. "I met him one night in front of headquarters. I asked him what the hell he was doing in a godforsaken place like New Guinea. He said, 'Actually, I'm enjoying flying a three-thousand-horsepower airplane. The only bad thing is missing the family.' I could tell that he meant it."

Charles cast a disapproving eye on some of the nose art that decorated the P-38s, said Rieman, and he was disgusted by evidence of American atrocities: beheaded Japanese, machine-gunned prisoners, garbage dumped on bodies, gold teeth yanked out of skulls. But he kept his opinions in his diary, maintained a low profile, and blended in easily with the men he lived and flew with.

"I remember on one occasion he was having a difficult time getting into formation," said Rieman. "Everybody was talking on the radio. Finally, somebody said, 'Hey, Lindy! Pull up your wheels. You're not flying the *Spirit of St. Louis*.' After the mission, everybody asked him what happened. He could've made up an excuse, like, 'The wheels were stuck.' But, no, he said, 'I forgot to pull them up.' That's being quite honest."

Forgetting to retract his wheels was the least of Lindbergh's worries that memorable day, July 28, 1944. He narrowly survived a head-on pass with a Japanese fighter, registering his first and only "kill" in the process. The two planes were closing on each other at a combined speed of almost six hundred miles per hour. "On that pass," he reflected, "elements of chance and skill interwove as in no other incident of my life."

When it began I had an advantage in altitude, and I was slightly diving, my enemy slightly climbing, when we opened fire. As we were flying directly at each other, there was no deflection to my aim or to his. Bullets streamed through the air like hail. I watched his wingspan widen in my gun sight as flashes rose from the bullet hits. When I could see the engine's cylinders, I released my gun trigger and pulled back on the control stick. The enemy plane pulled upward, too, to collide. I yanked back on the stick with all my strength, braced for the crash, felt a bump as we passed, but it was only air. I banked steeply in gaining altitude and saw below me the Japanese plane, out of control in a spiral dive toward the sea, twisting as it gathered speed. There was a splash and spray drifting. I felt I had approached so close to death that I could almost penetrate its mystery, that every time I saw life disappear I came closer to an essence that remained.

A few days later, Charles was caught out of position by a Zero during a dogfight. What saved him from being shot down were the enemy pilot's poor markmanship and the last-second intervention of MacDonald and Smith, who forced the Japanese fighter off with deflecting fire.

All told, Lindbergh went on fifty missions during his four months overseas, evenly divided between the Corsair and the P-38. He always downplayed his unofficial war record. One reason was that he had been a combatant in mufti. This was a severe and

Major Thomas McGuire and Lindbergh in 1944.

uncharacteristic breach of regulations for someone who had spent fifteen years as an officer in the Air Corps reserve and, his resignation notwithstanding, hoped to some day return. A lesser point was that airmen did not consider sorties flown in the Pacific theatre to be nearly as dangerous as those flown over Germany. (Rieman, for example, flew 164 missions, most of them self-described "milk runs.") By the time Lindbergh arrived in the Pacific, the skies were practically empty of enemy planes. "Any mission in the combat zone was called a combat mission," he acknowledged. "On some, the combat was intense; on others nonexistent. . . ." That said, surviving even one flight under fire, much less multiple missions, was an achievement to be quietly celebrated in any theatre of operations. A large number of skilled and brave pilots never returned from overseas. Among them was Thomas McGuire, who flew Lindbergh's wing on his first P-38 mission and became a good friend during their brief but intense time together.

Charles returned to the states in September 1944, tanned, trim, and happier than he had ever been to be in his family's embrace. By the following spring, both

Roosevelt and Hitler were dead and the war in Europe was over. Indicative of the new administration's attitude toward him, Lindbergh was one of a group of technical experts sent to inspect the missile and aircraft developments of conquered Germany.

The two-month trip was depressing. He saw many of his prewar fears realized. The Soviets had gobbled up a good chunk of Europe, filling a vacuum caused by Germany's defeat and the timidity of the war-weary Allies in dealing with the Communist colossus. Much of Western civilization had been razed by bombs: entire towns and villages, centuries-old cathedrals, irreplaceable works of art. Germany, which Charles had known as the world's most modern society in 1939, was simply unrecognizable rubble six years later. Tens of millions of men, women, and children had been slaughtered; a like number were now displaced, desperate for food, shelter, and order. The British Empire had disintegrated. America, as much by default as by choice, had become the protectorate of the free world, permanently embroiled in other nations' affairs.

Lindbergh was shown around Camp Dora, where slave laborers had been fed to the furnaces. While he agreed that the architects of Nazi genocide should be brought to trial, he refused to condemn Germany. No country's hands were clean, as the Allies' fire bombings of cities like Dresden and Tokyo—terror raids driven more by spite than strategy—made clear. "What is barbaric on one side of the earth is still barbaric on the other," he observed. "'Judge not that ye be not judged.' It is not the Germans alone, or the Japs, but the men of all nations to whom this war has brought shame and degradation."

In August 1945, the United States dropped atomic bombs on the Japanese cities of Hiroshima and Nagasaki, wiping out an aggregate 200,000 people with two simple, separate pushes of a button. On a much less lethal level, but with the same moral implications, Charles had felt the power of life and death in his own hand during bombing runs in the Pacific. "You press a button and death rains down. One second the bomb is hanging harmlessly in your racks, completely under your control. The next it is hurtling down through the air, and nothing in your power can revoke what you have done."

Lindbergh's experiences shook him to the core of his being. The chivalry that had characterized the fictional exploits of "Tam o' the Scoots" proved to be nonexistent in a climate of total war. The martial tradition of mutual respect among adversaries that he had expected to find had been replaced by unbridled contempt and unspeakable atrocities by all sides. He could never shake the images of the desecrated dead he had seen piled up in the Pacific and Germany, and for years he would pray for the soul of the anonymous Japanese pilot he had sent corkscrewing into the sea. One inconsequential but godlike encounter, plucked from a war that killed more than fifty million people around the world, encapsulated Lindbergh's growing moral dilemma—an internal tug-of-war between technology and the spiritual that would occupy the last part of his life.

It happened on one of his earliest missions. Swooping low over the coast of Japanese-held New Ireland, Charles spotted a man about a thousand yards off, wading through the surf—a legitimate target. He had the man in his sights . . . but then his trigger finger froze. He watched as his naked, weaponless foe, instead of trying to evade the shrieking metal pterodactyl bearing down on him, walked defiantly down the beach, determined to maintain his dignity even as he waited for the machine gun bullets to shred him to pieces.

Lindbergh zoomed past without firing.

"I shall never know who he was—Jap or native. But I realize that the life of this unknown stranger—probably an enemy—is worth a thousand times more to me than his death. I should never forgive myself if I had shot him—naked, courageous, defenseless, yet so unmistakably a man."

• • •

With the end of the war the Lindberghs entered their longest period of sustained domestication. After nearly two footloose decades, Anne was desperate to set down roots. The adventurous survey flights of just a few years earlier were no more, and there was a new addition to the family. Reeve, the Lindberghs' sixth and last child, was born October 2, 1945 at a New York hospital. With the world bled and bombed into exhaustion, even someone with Charles's storied wanderlust felt the need for blessed routine, at least temporarily.

While Charles was away in a war zone, Anne occupied herself with the children and in taking classes at the Cranbrook Academy of Art. She created this clay self-portrait in 1944.

Anne had grown to like Michigan, but business and family considerations predicated a move back east. In 1946, after briefly renting a house in Westport, Connecticut, the couple bought a secluded piece of wooded, waterfront property bordering on Scott's Cove, an arm of Long Island Sound. The site was near Darien, Connecticut, and just forty miles from Manhattan. The three-story stone-faced house had seven bedrooms and a second-floor playroom. There was plenty of space indoors and out for Jon, Land, Anne (nicknamed "Ansy" to avoid confusion with her mother), Scott, and Reeve to swim, wrestle, hike, shoot, sail, and fish—activities that their father delighted in teaching and supervising.

The children were loved, not pampered, and encouraged to explore just about anything that struck their fancy. As they got older, Charles would take them for airplane rides in a rented two-seater with dual controls. Only Jon, the eldest, actually got a pilot's license. (He also skydived.) But even he preferred the water to the sky, becoming an oceanographer and deep-sea diver. Charles didn't mind his children's disinterest in aviation. Like his father before him, he believed in guiding youngsters down life's paths, not shoving them.

Charles could be demanding and formal in his child-rearing. He insisted that he and Anne be addressed always as "Father" and "Mother," and he constantly preached the gospel of duty, responsibility, and accountability. He delivered lectures on such varied topics as the danger of watching *Howdy Doody*, the bogus sentimentality of Father's Day and Mother's Day, and the sheer waste of using paper napkins at the dining table. (He preferred to wipe his hands with his pocket handkerchief, a practice that his daughters considered gross.)

Obsessively organized, he employed a variety of checklists to keep his squadron of offspring flying straight. When he was home, each child was called into his study to discuss certain items listed under his or her name. Reeve got to where she could quickly size up a column and estimate how long she would be detained. "Were there many items in the column under my name, or just a few? And were they specific, tangible concerns, like 'rake left out in rain,' for which I could apologize and then leave the office, or were they of a more general nature, like 'reading comics' or 'chewing gum,' which would require discussion, and take more time? And woe betide me if there was something really big written on my list, like 'Freedom and Responsibility.' Freedom and Responsibility were good for half an hour, sometimes half an hour each."

The Lindbergh children attended public school before moving on to college. They turned out remarkably level-headed, considering that their famous father was always popping up in encyclopedias and social studies textbooks. "Your dad discovered America," a grade-school classmate once told one of the Lindbergh kids. "Yes," was the response, "and he flew across the ocean, too."

Lindbergh, resuming his gypsy lifestyle, crossed the ocean far more often than his family would have liked. One year alone he took eleven Atlantic trips and added a twelfth to the Pacific—and this didn't include his many domestic flights. He served as a special adviser to the U.S. Air Force (now a separate branch of the military), testing planes and inspecting bases on several continents. He was a consultant to the University of Chicago Ordnance Research Project. The top-secret CHORE committee evaluated the uses and effectiveness of missiles, bombs, machine guns, and other weapons. He also continued as an adviser to the commercial airline industry, evaluating planes, facilities, and service.

These obligations resulted in a highly irregular family life. Unlike other fathers who worked regular hours, Charles would be home for several days, during which time his personality dominated the household. ("This isn't a democracy," he liked to say, half-jokingly. "This is a beneficent dictatorship.") Then he would be gone for two or three weeks, off to some unpronounceable spot on the globe, before suddenly rematerializing for another short stay. His frequent and elongated absences gave Anne and the kids a chance to recuperate from his overpowering and often overbearing presence. But his company was missed at too many birthday celebrations, recitals, sporting events, holiday meals, and graduations.

"When my father was away, the energy vacuum was even greater than the verbal one," Reeve, one of his greatest defenders, later wrote. "I might not miss his lectures, but I missed his bounding up the stairs, skipping several of them on his way, and humming the shapeless, toneless tune that Anne, behind his back, called 'The Minnesota Funeral Dirge.' When he was absent there were no more family walks, no gatherings

In 1948–1949, Lindbergh made an around-the-world inspection tour of American air bases for the Air Force.

together in front of the living room fire while he read Rudyard Kipling's *The Jungle Book*, no evenings out on the porch watching weather, no sunsets and no storms. His physical absence also left us with an absence of physical parental affection, as he was always by far the more physically affectionate of our parents, though he would not allow this side of himself to show in public."

Charles continued to prefer not to show any side in public. He repeatedly turned down interview requests and shunned most social functions, finding awards dinners, testimonials, and the like to be well-intentioned affairs that were essentially pointless and consumed too much of his time. He did, however, show up at the Aero Club of Washington in 1949 to accept the Wright Brothers Memorial Trophy; five years later he received the equally prestigious Daniel Guggenheim Medal at a dinner in New York. Both awards honored his pioneering achievements in aviation. He also championed a select few private causes. One was working to preserve the memory and archives of Dr. Alexis Carrel, who died in occupied France in 1944; another was to see that the late Robert Goddard got the recognition due him as America embarked on the missile age.

As the 40s flowed into the 50s, Charles gradually returned to the good graces of his countrymen. He benefitted from the generally positive reviews he received for his 1948 book, *Of Flight and Life*, wherein the budding Cold Warrior argued that, despite the defeat of Nazi Germany, Western civilization was still under seige, this time from the godless Soviets. Revealing himself to be more humanistic and spiritual than previously portrayed, he confessed that, as a youth, "science was more important than either man or God. The one I took for granted; the other was too intangible for me to understand." Now, he had come to believe that "the quality of a civilization depends on a balance of body, mind, and spirit in its people, measured on a scale less human than divine." The book revolved around epiphanic moments he'd had during the war, including the time he'd lost consciousness during a high-altitude test flight, his near-fatal encounter with a Zero, and his postwar visit to Germany. Many Americans, learning of his war experiences for the first time, were willing to revise the harsh opinion they had formed of him during the America First controversy.

By the early 1950s a more involved literary project occupied most of his free time: an in-depth account of his flight to Paris. Charles was never happy with *We*, which had been written in a rush. He actually began work on what was to become *The Spirit of St. Louis* in 1938. Over the next fourteen years he worked on the manuscript whenever he had a few spare minutes: in a hut on a Pacific atoll . . . in a bomber returning from the North Pole . . . at the Army and Navy Club in Washington, D.C. . . . inside the family Ford while waiting out a traffic jam. Striving for the most accurate retelling of his flight and early life, he solicited the input of others. "Don't hesitate to be critical," he instructed Bud Gurney in early 1952, forwarding a copy of the work-in-progress. "I hope you like the chapters, but it is criticism that I need at this time. I have worked on the manuscript until my reactions to it are rather deadened. . . . From navigation to commas and general plan, any comments at all will be gratefully accepted and much appreciated."

The manuscript went through nearly a dozen drafts before reaching its final form. The narrative detailing his 1927 flight was written in the present tense, giving it an absorbing, immediate feel. The central story was interleaved with flashbacks sketching the key personalities and events that ultimately placed him in the cockpit of the *Spirit of St. Louis*, challenging the Atlantic. Like *"We,"* the 600-page book ended with his triumphant landing in Paris.

The Spirit of St. Louis was published by Scribner's in 1953 after first being serialized in the *Saturday Evening Post* for a record $100,000. It was a publishing sensation, garnering universally favorable reviews and selling several hundred thousand copies its first year. Anne, whom Charles always championed as the real writer in the family, had worked very closely with him on the book. He dedicated it "To A. M. L.—Who will never realize how much of this book she has written."

Actually, Anne had an excellent idea of her contribution, which induced a mix of happiness and jealousy when it was announced a few months later that *The Spirit of St. Louis* had been awarded the 1954 Pulitzer Prize for biography. "I helped him write the book," she told herself. "I helped it be that perfect. I know it never would have been that perfect without my help." But she also gave Charles his due. He had written "his" book. What she really envied was Charles's ability to bring purpose, focus, and action to everything he tackled, whether it was flying a plane, working in the laboratory, writing a manuscript, or simply ascertaining the best buy on a household appliance.

About the time Charles was awarded the Pulitzer, he received an even more gratifying honor. Fourteen years after he had last worn his wings, he had his commission restored, by order of President Dwight D. Eisenhower. On April 7, 1954, Lindbergh was sworn in as a brigadier general in the U.S. Air Force Reserve. This put him in occasional contact with actor James Stewart, who had flown bombers over Germany and remained in the reserves after the war. When *The Spirit of St. Louis* was released as a movie three years later, Stewart played the role of his boyhood idol. The film died

The Lindberghs made few public appearances in the immediate postwar period. On January 25, 1954, however, Charles (seated second from right on the dais) received the prestigious Daniel Guggenheim Medal for "pioneering achievement in flight and air navigation" at a dinner of the Institute of the Aeronautical Sciences at New York's Astor Hotel. To the immediate left of Lindbergh is old friend and philanthropist Harry Guggenheim.

at the box office, but not before Reeve Lindbergh delivered the best line. She accompanied Anne to a showing at the Radio City Music Hall in New York. During one particularly suspenseful moment, the eleven-year-old turned to her mother and anxiously asked, "Does he make it?"

For years, Anne had been wondering the same thing about her marriage. Could she and Charles make it? Now together almost thirty years, she had grown weary of being viewed principally as an appendage to her husband—a lonely, unfulfilled appendage at that. His frequent absences exacerbated the emotional void that she often felt even in the midst of his overpowering and overly critical presence. He was a man of many superior qualities, she admitted, but he seemed incapable of providing the understanding, support, and emotional intimacy she craved. She could never forget—or understand—how Charles went through the entire ordeal of their son's kidnapping without once weeping over their shared loss.

That some admirers of *The Spirit of St. Louis* had hailed its author as another Antoine de Saint-Exupery struck Anne as being almost blasphemous. In her mind there was only one "St-Ex." and he had perished during a reconaissance flight over southern France in 1944. A few years earlier, she had spent time with the author of

Three pioneers of aviation—Jimmy Doolittle, Harry Guggenheim, and Lindbergh—in 1959.

The Little Prince and *Wind, Sand and Stars,* and her infatuation was so obvious that even her normally preoccupied husband could not help but notice. Although her unusually long diary entries describing those days fell short of saying so, here perhaps was the person she should have married—a soul mate ("tall and stooped and a little bald") who seemed to understand her needs as a woman and an artist.

Anne was no churchmouse, no matter what her nonthreatening size and demeanor suggested. But few women in that pre-feminist era could have avoided being smothered by the supernormal self-assuredness that was Charles Lindbergh. Her despondency caused her to look for answers with the Freudian pyschiatrist who was restoring the confidence and mental stability of her brother, Dwight, who had struggled for decades with intermittent bouts of severe depression. Anne's sessions with Dr. John Rosen lasted less than two years. Emboldened by Rosen's sympathetic insights, she began to assert herself, which drove a deeper wedge between her and Charles. Lindbergh was so upset by the idea of his wife spilling out her innermost feelings and thoughts to a virtual stranger that he moved out of their bedroom and refused to speak to her for weeks.

Anne believed in duty above all else, and her principal duty was to Charles, despite his often careless treatment of her. As the years rolled by, her social life continued to revolve around her children, a growing brood of grandchildren, and the close circle of artists, writers, musicians, publishers, and other friends that descended on Darien whenever her husband was gone.

At the same time Charles was finishing *The Spirit of St. Louis*, Anne was channeling her churning emotions into a tour de force of her own: a series of connected essays that examined the plight of the modern housewife and mother. For several winters she had spent a week or so on the beaches of Florida's west coast, giving her mind and emotions a chance to roam. The exquisitely detailed seashells that washed up on shore captivated her. With her artist's eye she saw how each variety of shell—the double-sunrise, the oyster, the argonauta, and so on—could serve as a metaphor for the cycles of a woman's life.

Gift from the Sea was an internal quest for harmony that argued for a woman's right to live her own life within the traditional framework of marriage. This necessarily entailed solitude: time for introspection and time to explore one's creative side. No radical feminist tract, the book concluded that marriage and family, despite being imperfect institutions, are worthy of being preserved. "Security in a relationship lies neither in looking back to what it was in nostalgia nor forward to what it might be in dread or anticipation, but living in

Anne and Land in 1941 and then in the late 1950s. Land became a rancher in Montana while Anne wrote children's books.

the present relationship and accepting it as it is now, within their limits. . . ."

Gift from the Sea (which her editors at Pantheon Press wanted to title *The Mass of Men Lead Lives of Quiet Desperation*), was released in March 1955. At less than a hundred pages, Anne and her publisher expected only modest sales. Instead, it spent more than a year on top of the best-seller list and would go on to sell a combined 2.6 million copies in hardcover and paperback—a phenomenal showing that once again made Anne Morrow Lindbergh the country's favorite female author. Nearly a half-century later, the book continues to sell at the rate of several thousand copies a year.

Apart from making them richer and, in Anne's case, providing a form of catharsis, *The Spirit of St. Louis* and *Gift from the Sea* helped the authors reclaim their reputations, which had been damaged by the furor over their prewar activities. In the midst of this period of professional kudos, public redemption, and private angst, each suffered through the loss of their mother.

The Lindberghs' fifth child, Scott, was born in 1943. Several years later he was pictured chopping kindling outside the family's Swiss chalet.

For several years after the war, Charles and Anne occasionally made extended trips with the children to Detroit, usually by train, to see the family matriarch. Evangeline had retired from teaching in 1942, just as the first signs of Parkinson's disease were becoming evident. Reeve recalled the final mother-and-son reunion inside Evangeline's home shortly before her death one September day in 1954. "She smiled at my father, from her bed, with lingering tenderness. The look that passed between those two was so loving that even I could feel the nature of it, and was calmed."

Evangeline was buried in the family plot at Pine Lake Cemetery. Her brother Charles, always Lindbergh's favorite uncle, was invited to move into the big house in Connecticut. There was plenty of room now that the older boys, Jon and Land, were studying at Stanford. Reeve remembered "moments of head-shaking exasperation" over the eccentric old bachelor, who for years had entertained the children inside his Detroit laboratory. "My father was especially concerned about the inventions: toothpaste that we were forbidden to try because of its possible toxicity, car polish that took the paint off the fender of one of the family cars when Uncle applied it. . . ." Then there were Uncle Charles's dirty jokes, which regularly embarrassed family members and guests. "I did not understand them," she admitted, "but nonetheless knew that I was to 'overlook' Uncle's stories." Uncle Charles ultimately joined relatives

Jon became a record-setting deep-sea diver.

in Florida, where he lived out his days.

A few months after Evangeline's passing, Anne's mother died after suffering a stroke. "No matter how much one is prepared for death of one's parents by age or illness," Anne wrote a friend, "it does not lighten the blow of tangible separation. . . . It is a great wrench and a great testing of all our powers and faith. . . ."

While Evangeline bequeathed $50,000 to be divided equally between her son and her brother, Betty Morrow left a substantial $9.4-million estate. Anne received $50,000 cash and life interest in trust of one-third of the estate, which remained sizable after all of her mother's generous charitable bequests were made. The inheritances, coupled with the windfall from their books (Charles sold the

Lindbergh with the last of his six children, Reeve, at her 1968 wedding. "By habit and self-discipline, as long as I knew him, he tried to hide even the happiest moments of his family life from curious eyes," she wrote of her father in her memoir, *Under a Wing.* **"It was as if the very act of admitting family happiness, exposing it to public view, would somehow destroy it, as it had been destroyed once before."**

movie rights to *Spirit* for $200,000 plus ten percent of the gross receipts), had little appreciable impact on Charles's and Anne's lifestyles. Now in their fifties, they were already well off, lived unostentatiously, and were always looking for ways to shed, not gain, material possessions. Most of the money went into the children's already healthy trust funds, which they could start drawing on once they reached twenty-one.

Evangeline's death marked the end of Charles's longstanding Detroit connections. Lacking any compelling reason to visit, he never returned to his hometown in the twenty years following his mother's funeral.

Betty Morrow's death helped free Anne to commit the ultimate act of defiance, one that would have been unthinkable to her mother, who had been a happy wife and devoted widow. In 1956, Anne began an affair with her longtime physician that lasted several years. Dr. Dana Atchley was kindly, intelligent, and mired in an unhappy marriage of his own. Fourteen years older than Anne, he had nursed her through a miscarriage and a gall bladder operation in the late 1940s. Now he was her almost constant social companion, their rendezvous occurring at a two-room apartment Anne rented in Manhattan. If Charles was aware of his wife's adultery, he never let on. According to their daughter Ansy, "He knew that Mother loved him and would never leave him. And that was all he needed to know."

JIMMY STEWART

"Lucky to be Lindy"

In the spring of 1957, Warner Brothers released the film version of Lindbergh's flight. *The Spirit of St. Louis* was directed by Billy Wilder and starred Jimmy Stewart in the lead role. Stewart, a decorated bomber pilot during World War II, had always been an admirer of the Lone Eagle, as he made clear in a *Collier's* article.

"Who's Lindbergh? And what's the *Spirit of St. Louis?*" That's what my ten-year-old boy asked me when I came home with the news that I was going to play Lindbergh. It was a jolt to realize that a whole new generation was growing up that had never heard of him.

When Charles A. Lindbergh electrified the world with his flight from New York to Paris in 1927, I was in my teens and I like to think I was one of his first all-out supporters and admirers. So when producer Leland Hayward asked me to play Lindbergh in *The Spirit of St. Louis,* I didn't ask for details. I simply said: "When do we start shooting?"

I first saw Lindbergh's picture in the local newspaper of my home town, Indiana, Pennsylvania. The caption merely said he planned to fly the Atlantic alone in a single-engined plane. That clipping was the beginning of my Lindbergh scrapbook. When I was laid low with scarlet fever, I combed the newspapers day after day for more details. Then I carved out a model of the *Spirit of St. Louis* and asked my father for a larger piece of beaverboard.

I drew on it a map of the North Atlantic. On one side I crayoned a silhouette of the Woolworth Building, to symbolize New York,

Jimmy Stewart as the Lone Eagle.

and in Europe I drew the Eiffel Tower, to identify Paris. Then I bent the beaverboard in a semicircle to show the curvature of the earth, and tacked the model of Lindbergh's plane over the drawing of the Woolworth Building.

I had carefully charted the course Lindbergh had said he would take, figured his speed, and where he would be every hour during his flight. The day before he took off, I got out of bed and went down to my father's store, cleared

out the window, and put the map on display with an announcement saying the *Spirit of St. Louis* would be placed in Lindbergh's approximate position every hour during the flight.

From the moment he took off from New York and landed in Paris 33½ hours later, I don't think I got any more sleep than Lindbergh did. Lindbergh's problem was staying awake; mine was staying asleep that Friday night while he was unreported over the

Atlantic between Newfoundland and Ireland.

I was at my father's store at dawn on Saturday and moved the plane to the southern tip of Ireland, where he had just been reported. As other stores opened for business and farmers began coming to town for weekend shopping, people gathered in front of my display as though it were a World Series scoreboard. By noon you couldn't fight your way into my father's store. I imagine my father lost a lot of business that day, but he never said a word to me about it. In fact, he was rather proud of what I had done.

Months later, while Lindbergh was on his triumphal tour, I journeyed the forty-seven miles to Pittsburgh in the hopes of getting an autograph, but the crowds were so immense I barely caught a glimpse of him. Bitterly disappointed, I returned home and it wasn't until a few months ago that I caught up with him. We had dinner together to discuss my portrayal of him in the movie. However, it seemed a little late to ask for his autograph!

After Leland had bought the screen rights to The Spirit of St. Louis to produce it for Warner Brothers, he thought it would be a good idea for Lindbergh and director Billy Wilder to meet. A few months later, Lindbergh called from a Pasadena hotel and agreed to come to Wilder's home in Beverly Hills at 4:00 P.M. the following Sunday. Leland's wife suggested they stop by the Pasadena hotel to pick Lindbergh up but Leland laughed at the idea. "He must have fifty cars and chauffeurs at his disposal," Leland told her. So they drove straight to Wilder's house.

Lindbergh rang the front door-

Paris is a knothole in this still from the 1957 movie, *The Spirit of St. Louis*.

bell at 4:03 P.M.—three minutes late—apologizing profusely for his tardiness. He had come twenty miles by streetcar and bus, then walked to Wilder's house. He had calculated his arrival time to the minute. But those four blocks from the bus stop to Wilder's house were five times as long as the street map indicated, Lindbergh explained apologetically.

"Why didn't you tell us you had no car available?" Wilder asked, incredulously.

"Oh," replied Lindbergh, "I *like* to ride on a bus."

During the filming, Lindbergh was a stickler for detail. His barnstorming pal, Bud Gurney, a technical advisor on the film, checked out every scene. Sometimes Wilder had to phone Lindbergh anyway—for instance, did he wear cotton in his ears during the flight? Lindbergh said he did.

Only once did Lindbergh himself visit us on location during the shooting of the picture. We were on Long Island, New York, taking landing shots with an exact replica

of the *Spirit of St. Louis*. He turned up unannounced one afternoon. Lindbergh asked pilot Stan Reaver all about the performance details of the substitute *Spirit of St. Louis*—which was built from the same plans as the original—and expressed nostalgic satisfaction when he learned that its flying characteristics also matched the original.

When Reaver was ordered to take the plane up for a final landing shot, Lindbergh warned him: "Don't forget to sideslip her in for a perfect three-point landing. Remember, I'm supposed to be flying that plane."

Lindbergh wasn't kidding, either. When it came to flying scenes, he would settle for nothing less than perfection. And we all did our best to give it to him.

Well, my kids know who Lindbergh is now. And they're flying a model of the *Spirit of St. Louis*. As for me, I'm lucky to be Lindy.

The Philippines, 1970: One lone eagle meets another.

Birds, Not Planes

Was civilization progress? By the 1960s, with society and the natural world both undergoing seismic changes, Charles Lindbergh was convinced that it was not.

The obvious case in point was aviation. Less than forty years after his harrowing flight to Paris, flying had become safe, dull, and predictable—a condition that guaranteed a fall-off in his interest. The poetry of imagination had taken a back seat to technological innovation. Even before the war, the French aviation bard Joseph Kessel was lamenting that planes ("organisms"), once as unique as human beings, were now standardized "flying torpedoes that have nothing to do with flying and turn the pilot amid all his buttons and dials into a sort of accountant." It had grown exponentially worse. The commercial airline industry had homogenized the travel experience for pilots and passengers, replacing adventure and discovery with safety, convenience, and comforting familiarity.

Far more troubling to Lindbergh was aviation's devastating effect on the environment. He regretted the part he had played in nature's despoiling. "The primitive was at the mercy of the civilized in our twentieth-century times," he observed candidly, "and nothing had made it more so than the airplane I had helped develop. I had helped to change the environment of our lives."

Lindbergh's doubts caused him to oppose the supersonic passenger jets being considered by U.S. airlines in the early sixties. Ultimately, Pan Am (on whose board he served) and other domestic carriers decided not to build an American version of the Anglo-French Concorde (though their decision was based more on financial considerations than Lindbergh's warnings against noise and atmospheric pollution). In 1964, he crystalized his thoughts in a *Reader's Digest* article describing his recent trip to Kenya. His soul was opened by the primitive romance of the "dark continent," where he observed the environment and customs of the warrior society of the Masai.

"Lying under an acacia tree," he wrote, "with the sounds of dawn around me, I realized more clearly, in fact, what man should never overlook: that the construction of an airplane, for instance, is simple when compared with the evolutionary achievement of a bird; that airplanes depend upon advanced civilization; and that where civilization is most advanced, few birds exist.

"I realized that if I had to choose, I would rather have birds than airplanes."

Charles had loved the outdoors since his boyhood days in Minnesota, developing an appreciation for the rhythms and nuances of the natural world. His survival skills could shame most modern men and would remain top-notch to the very end of his life. But his priorities evolved. For example, anxious to test his courage and marksmanship on a big-game safari, he quickly decided to put down his rifle. What was the point? He wasn't Grandfather Lindbergh tramping the Minnesota wilderness, or a Masai warrior needing an animal's flesh for sustenance and the creature's skin for clothing. He had once thought that confronting a wild animal in the brush was one of the last authentic tests of individual courage left to man. But the lions, rhinonoceros, and hippopotamuses he came across were too majestic and too dignified to arbitrarily slay. He came to believe that killing in the name of sport was murder. He had seen enough death in his day.

Lindbergh's wide range of environmental activities in the sixties and early seventies deserves its own book. Whether it was fighting to save the blue whale in Peru, the one-horned Jacan rhinoceros in Indonesia, or the monkey-eating eagle in the Philippines, he brought the same kind of missionary zeal to the causes of conservation that he had previously applied to aviation. He became a powerful spokesman for several organizations in the ecology movement, including the World Wildlife Fund, The Nature Conservancy, The Oceanic Foundation, and the International Union for the Conservation of Nature and Natural Resources.

"If I were entering adulthood now instead of in the environment of fifty years ago, I would choose a career that kept me in touch with nature more than science," he wrote in the Christmas 1967 issue of *Life*. "This is the choice an individual can still make—but no longer mankind in general. Too few natural areas remain; both by intent and indifference we have insulated ourselves from the wilderness that produced us. Our emphasis on science has resulted in an alarming rise in world populations, the demand and ever-increasing emphasis of science to improve their standards and maintain their vigor. I have been forced to the conclusion that an over-emphasis of science weakens character and upsets life's essential balance."

Sadly for Anne, the same sort of balance was not evident in their domestic situation. In 1963, eighteen-year-old Reeve entered Radcliffe, the last of the children to leave home. Looking to downsize their lives, Charles and Anne sold the house and built a five-room cottage elsewhere on the property. It was designed and furnished along simple, unadorned lines, though—reflecting Charles's mounting concerns over the threat of nuclear war—it included an elaborate $20,000 bomb shelter.

The children were all making careers and families of their own. Jon, the oldest, earned his biology degree from Stanford in 1954, married a classmate, and the following year produced the Lindberghs' first grandchild. After serving as a Navy frogman, Jon stayed on the West Coast and distinguished himself in deep-sea diving and oceanography. He appeared on the cover of *Life* and in a few episodes of the television series *Sea Hunt*, none of which pleased his father. In 1962 he made a record-breaking dive of 49 hours at 432 feet off the Bahamas, just one of the many "wet and dangerous" activities he was regularly involved in.

Land, who had spent summers on western ranches, followed his brother to Stanford and also married a college classmate. He settled in Montana, where he operated a large cattle ranch. Ansy—sweet, reserved and shy—went to Radcliffe and the Sorbonne. After graduating, she married a Frenchman, had two children, and began writing children's books. Reeve would pursue teaching and writing after her own

Lindbergh, a brigadier general in the reserves, traveled to Vietnam in 1967.

graduation from Radcliffe, marrying a photographer in 1968 and settling in Vermont.

The "wayward" Lindbergh child was the absentminded and stubborn Scott, who, growing up, often bore the brunt of Charles's lectures and verbal dressing-downs. Scott loved fast cars, moved to France, married a much older woman, and thought he might like to dedicate his life to studying animal behavior. He could have started with his father, who was so incensed over his youngest son's irresponsibility that he quit communicating with him for years and wrote him out of his will.

During the 1960s Charles and Anne bought a chalet overlooking Lake Geneva in Switzerland. They also built a house on the Hawaiian island of Maui. The chalet was a convenient gathering spot for family members in Europe, especially since Ansy and Scott were living in France. The Hawaiian property, which Charles bought from Sam Pryor, an old friend and Pan Am executive, was far less accessible. Its remoteness, coupled with the lush beauty, naturally made the four-acre site irresistable to Lindbergh. "There is nothing quite comparable when you think of waterfalls, natural swimming pools, and the ocean beyond," he said. Charles built a simple stone structure with no modern amenities, an Edenlike retreat where he and Anne could hopefully rediscover the fundamentals of living and loving. They began by spending one or two months a year there. Eventually they made it their legal residence, but Charles would die before his ambition to live there permanently was realized.

Anne, whose affair with Dana Atchley had run its course, had come to terms with their unconventional marriage, and with life in general. Real happiness, she had decided, was transitory at best. The best one could hope for was to recognize those fleeting moments of joy and fulfillment and squeeze them for all that they were worth. She

On March 20, 1968, Lindbergh made his first public speech in more than a decade, addressing the Alaska legislature about the need for conservation.

and Charles spent an aggregate of only a few months of each year together, and sometimes not even that much. Once he told Anne that he had to take a short trip to the Pacific. "A month?" she asked. "Oh, no," he said. "Just Hawaii and the Philippines— and then back around the world the other way." Their paths crossed at their children's homes on both sides of the Atlantic, and they rendezvoused at their various houses and vacation spots. But for the most part, Charles—unencumbered by financial worries and tied to few familial responsibilities and professional obligations—led as free, footloose, and varied a lifestyle as any hippie of the period could hope for.

He was at Cape Kennedy in December 1968 for the launch of Apollo VIII's mission to the moon (astronaut Frank Borman carried a picture of Lindbergh with him inside the capsule), and again the following July when Apollo XI realized Robert Goddard's dream of a moon landing. The media naturally drew comparisons between Neil Armstrong, the first man to walk on the moon, and the man who had flown to Paris forty-two years earlier. And just as naturally, Charles refused to cooperate with the press, preferring to keep the world's spotlight off him and on the three astronauts, where he felt it belonged.

When Charles wasn't working on his own literary projects (his *Wartime Journals* was published to mixed reviews in 1970), he was assisting authors researching biographies of his father, Dr. Alexis Carrel, and Goddard. He also arranged for the publication of John Nance's book, *The Gentle Tasaday: A Stone Age People in the Philippine Rain Forest,* and wrote the foreword.

Lindbergh's March 1972 expedition to the caves of the "gentle Tasaday" was the most gratifying of the several environmental rescue missions he made to the Philippines. On an earlier trip he had made the acquaintance of a young Filipino politician named

A hero to everyone in the American space program, Lindbergh obligingly signs autographs for the Apollo astronauts at the White House in 1968.

Manuel Elizalde Jr., who administrated the affairs of tribal minorities for President Ferdinand Marcos. The stone-age Tasaday, who had no recorded history, apparently had been living in the rain forest of Mindanao Island for centuries without any contact with the outside world. The peaceful people practiced no religion and had no words for war. Then developers threatened their existence, until Elizalde enlisted Lindbergh's assistance. The world's most prominent freelance environmentalist eagerly came to the Tasaday's aid. Along with several much younger companions, Charles jumped from a hovering helicopter onto a 100-foot-high platform built in the impenetrable jungle—a remarkable maneuver, considering Charles had just turned seventy.

Over the next month Charles, Elizalde and their band lived amongst the Tasaday. Charles, dubbed "Kakay Shalo," was indefatiguable in the saunalike, leech-infested surroundings. He gratefully accepted grubs as snack food. "Was not this a twentieth-century Garden of Eden?" he asked himself as he lay in his sleeping bag at night, listening to the patter of rain on his tent. "I had never seen a happier people. My instinct drew me toward the Tasaday; my intellect toward civilization." The international publicity Charles helped whip up proved to be both good and bad. President Fernando Marcos ordered that a 46,000-acre preserve be created, but over time tribe members, exposed to their first taste of modern life, began drifting towards the bright lights of civilization.

Some critics have since concluded that the entire Tasaday story was a hoax fabricated by Elizalde and Marcos, who were facing elections. If true, it may explain why Lindbergh never returned to the Philippines after paying a second visit to the Tasaday that May. Nothing could spoil his visceral memories of the place, however. "At times,"

In the fall of 1968, Charles and Anne attended the dinner of the National Institute of Social Sciences in New York where they received gold medals for their "distinguished service to humanity."

he wrote after an impromptu sleepover on the beach in Luzon, "I feel like abandoning modern life. No going-to-bed procedure is required—no washing dishes, locking doors, opening windows, turning down sheets, not even undressing. You walk to your shelter, lie down on a grass mat, and look upward at the stars. The glow of campfire embers warms your face. You hear rippling surf, rustling leaves. Smoke from driftwood chips traces through the weedy smell of ocean. Your body's usual movements contour the sand to fit your bones. You have time to think, to become aware of your awareness."

• • •

Back in civilization, Lindbergh remained neurotically private, packing his disguise of beret and glasses when traveling and leaving in a huff whenever he was recognized. On one occasion in Paris, a young woman with a sketch pad approached his table while he, Anne, and friends were dining. Lindbergh insisted that they leave the restaurant.

Anne at her writing desk in 1969.

"The kid was only trying to earn a few francs," one of his dinner companions said. "What harm was she doing?"

"She might have drawn us and sold the drawing to the newspapers," Lindbergh answered.

Outside of intermittent visits with family members, Charles preferred his superficially maintained network of acquaintances strung out around the world. Past the age where most men are content to draw Social Security and watch television, he remained open to new sensations. Anne believed he had an affair with an attractive Filipina, and rumors swirled around his longtime relationship with a buxom blonde stewardess who shared his interest in the metaphysical. In each instance the woman was young enough to be his granddaughter. Whether platonic or sexual, the chief attraction of these relationships was that they didn't demand a long-term commitment. In this, there seemed to be no difference between the schoolboy who had shuttled between households in three states and the aging activist who barnstormed between continents. As Anne saw it, Charles Lindbergh never stopped fleeing intimacy. But his ceaseless, almost frantic, tramping around the planet would soon come to a halt.

Back from the Philippines, he developed a series of coughs and fevers that affected his always healthy appetite and caused him to lose weight. Too weak to travel much, he worked with Anne on shaping her diaries and letters into publishable form. The first volume, covering her college years prior to meeting Charles, was published as

Lindbergh hugs Philippines minority chief Datu Ma Falen during a visit in 1970 to the settlements of the Ubu tribe on the island of Mindanao. He is carrying an M-16 rifle because of trouble in the area at the time.

Lindbergh's first plane, which he purchased for $500 in April 1923, was found decades later inside a barn and shipped back east. Excited over the find, Lindbergh traveled to Long Island for a nostalgic reunion and to offer advice on restoring it to its original condition. Here the Curtiss JN-4 "Jenny" passes the presidential reviewing stand during the 1977 inaugural parade for President Jimmy Carter.

Bring Me a Unicorn. A second collection, this time detailing their early years of marriage up through their son's kidnapping, *Hour of Gold, Hour of Lead*, was in the works and would be released in 1973. Three more volumes eventually would follow, after which Anne would write no more books.

In late 1972, Charles entered Columbia-Presbyterian Hospital in New York for a checkup and was unexpectedly diagnosed with lymphatic cancer. In January, four days before his seventy-first birthday, he began radiation therapy. The cancer went into remission, and over the next several months, much of it spent on Maui, he regained most of his weight and wanderlust. His future travel plans, however, were dashed when he fell ill again in the late spring of 1973. Once again he rebounded, but never to the level of energy he and others were accustomed to. He began thinking of his mortality. He had never been a particularly nostalgic person. But several times he dropped in on an old friend in Washington, slipping into the Smithsonian Institution to take a long, silent look at the *Spirit of St. Louis* hanging in the gallery.

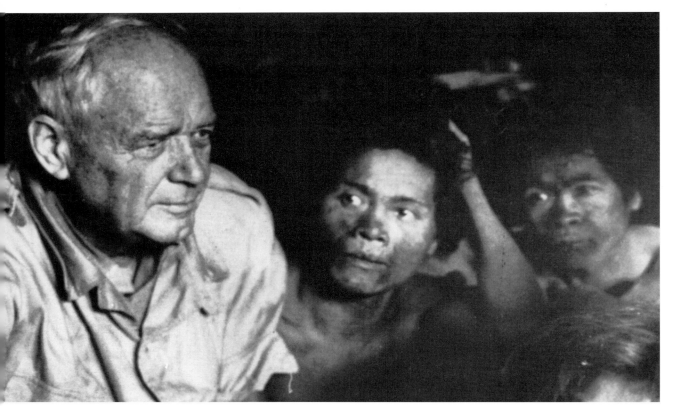

Lindbergh sits beside two Tasady in their cave in a southern Philippines rain forest during his 1972 expedition. He described his week-long stay with the primitive tribe as "one of the great experiences of life."

By the following spring the cancer had returned in full force. Drugs, blood transfusions, and chemotherapy could not arrest it. By the end of July, there was nothing his doctors could do. Charles quietly and methodically began putting his affairs in order. He lay in the hospital's intensive care unit while his children, told for the first time of his condition, rushed from all corners of the map to be by his side. He had a touching rapprochement with Scott, who flew in from France despite being sick himself with hepatitis.

Charles was not afraid of death. He had faced it on too many occasions, and pondered its mysteries far too often, for him not to consider it the ultimate adventure. Despite the pain and his weakened condition, he was determined to be in control until the very end. He would not die inside the artificial and antiseptic environment of some New York hospital. He wanted to draw his last breaths in the isolated serenity of Maui. When his doctors refused to give him written permission to make such an arduous trip, Lindbergh arranged through Sam Pryor to be secretly flown there, on a stretcher, in the curtained-off first-class section of a United Air Lines jet.

He arrived on August 17, 1974, and was moved into a small rented cottage, near Hana, that his Hawaiian doctor had arranged for in advance. It sat on a hill, surrounded by lush foliage and overlooking the Pacific. He was attended by Anne, his sons, and two around-the-clock nurses. Over the next several days, as infections,

Lindbergh in 1973, just a year before his death. "Mortality is an illusion of the minds of men, a figment of reason," he mused in the autobiography he was working on at the time. "I am past as well as present."

Tourists stand by Lindbergh's grave in a remote Hawaiian cemetery. After his death, "there was an element of relief in his absence, some quietness that we had not ever known in our lives before," the aviator's daughter, Reeve Lindbergh, reflected years later. "But he left behind a vast hole in our universe, as great as the death of a star."

pneumonia, and the cancer ravaged his body, Charles assumed the duties of funeral director. He didn't want to be embalmed. That was unnatural. He wanted to be placed in a simple coffin as quickly as possible after he died, dressed in work clothes and wrapped in his favorite Hudson's Bay blanket. He supervised the digging of a grave (large enough to eventually accommodate Anne) in the yard of an old missionary church, overlooking Kipahulu Bay, that he and Pryor had helped restore.

Land worried that some of his father's requests might get the family into legal trouble. Lindbergh smiled.

"That's your problem," he said. "I won't be here."

• • •

During his seventy-two years, Charles Lindbergh led a life that was remarkable for its breadth and depth of physical and intellectual vigor. Like all people, great or small, he had his contradictions. Foremost was his relationship with the media—and, by extension, the public. He professed to hate the press, yet he was never afraid to use the media as a megaphone when it suited him. John Lardner, for one, claimed that "Lindbergh was deliberately responsible for his continuing fame and notoriety.

Photo Credits

Index